NELSON
MANDELA

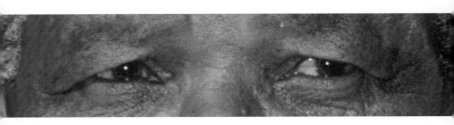

POCKET
GIANTS

COLIN
BUNDY

The History Press

Cover image © Mary Evans Picture Library.

First published 2015

The History Press
The Mill, Brimscombe Port
Stroud, Gloucestershire, GL5 2QG
www.thehistorypress.co.uk

British Library Cataloguing in Publication Data.
A catalogue record for this book is available from the British Library.

ISBN 978 0 7509 5920 9

Typesetting and origination by The History Press
Printed in Malta by Melita Press

NELSON MANDELA

POCKET
GIANTS

Contents

Introduction

It's impossible to make small talk with an icon
Which is why, to find my tongue,
I stare down at those crunched-up
One-time boxer's knuckles.
In their flattened pudginess I find
Something partly reassuring,
Something slightly troubling,
Something, at least, not transcendent.

Jeremy Cronin, 1997[1]

The South African cartoonist Zapiro celebrated Nelson Mandela's eightieth birthday with a scene called 'Nelson Mandela: The Early Years'. An African primary school teacher, holding sheets of paper her tiny wards have handed in, confides to a colleague: 'This one can't make up his mind: he put down "lawyer, activist, freedom fighter, prisoner of conscience, president, reconciler, nation-builder, visionary and 20th century icon".' Zapiro's homage not only provides a thumbnail sketch of a famous career but also hints at the dilemma confronting anyone writing a short biography of the man. So many aspects of Mandela's life are familiar that they challenge a biographer to find fresh meaning in them: the rural childhood, an early adulthood shaped by opposition to apartheid, a watershed decision to take up arms, a famous trial and a life sentence; and after twenty-seven years in jail, a remarkable policy of reconciliation and his election as the first president of democratic South Africa.

Consider, too, the quite extraordinary veneration and affection he won from people across the world – never more obvious than in the torrent of tributes and avalanche of encomia that greeted his death. How does any observer sift the actual life of an individual from the idealised hero:

a secular saint, symbol not only of his own nation's rebirth but moral leader of humankind, whose death reminded a world of its hunger for hope, for a better future? How does one trace the tentative steps, mistakes and mishaps, the flaws and failures which are the lot of any human life from an air-brushed, formulaic, eulogised life-story that seems to transcend mortal measures?

There is an element of retrieval involved in a posthumous Mandela biography, however brief: an attempt to rescue the man from the myth. After all, what was the legacy of the man who died in December 2013? Those who rushed to wrap themselves in Mandela's mantle included Havana and the White House, Israelis and Palestinians, the Vatican and ayatollahs, Chinese government and China's dissidents – and countless others across every political spectrum. Does any death so universally mourned not require a life and its achievements to have been universalised and sanitised, stripped of complexity, hallowed *and* hollowed, remade as an identikit icon? And if so, the challenge is to arrive at a biographical narrative that recognises Mandela as a compelling and complex political actor, but subject to the kinds of constraints and contradictions that describe any career.

So this biography locates Mandela in his time and place, indicating the social and political currents that bore him. It reminds readers of a point made frequently by Mandela himself: that his own achievements were part of broader, collective efforts – and that they cannot be otherwise understood. And it shows that his political efforts and those of the African National Congress (which he served for seventy years) involved the compromises, short cuts and shortcomings that are intrinsic to any politics in a complex world.

To write a biography that eschews hagiography is not an attempt to belittle Nelson Mandela, nor to carry out some sort of hatchet job on his reputation. Mandela's stature as a 'giant' is beyond question. As nationalist leader, his place in his country's history is comparable to those of Atatürk, Nasser, Nehru, Nkrumah, Sukarno and Ho Chi Minh; as exemplar of moral and civic virtues, he ranks with Lincoln, Gandhi and Martin Luther King (although he did not share the last two's adherence to non-violence as a principle); as a twentieth-century public figure who inspired love and respect, he belonged to a tiny club including perhaps Pope John XXIII, Mother Teresa and the Dalai Lama. Mandela – observed J.M. Coetzee – was, by the time of his death, universally held to be a great man: 'he may well be the last of the great men, as the concept of greatness retires into the historical shadows.'[2]

Yet the conundrum persists: how much of his towering reputation derived directly from Mandela-the-man, his principles and practice, his deeds and words – and how much was the product of a constructed version, Mandela-the-myth, an image deliberately burnished for political purposes? It is worth reflecting that Mandela's place in history is guaranteed by his role after his release in February 1990; the man who walked into the transfixed gaze of the global media that Sunday afternoon was already a legend. He was the world's most famous political prisoner; he was absent, yet imminently present; his silence reverberated. He had 'acquired an almost posthumous eminence',[3] showered with honorary degrees and prizes.

How does one explain so singular a renown? In order to answer this question, this biography does not begin with Mandela's childhood and then trace his life throughout ninety-five years; instead, it commences with a history of Mandela-the-myth, the making of the icon, and then resumes the more conventional form of a life history.

1

Man and Myth: The Construction of an Icon

21 years in captivity
Are you so blind that you cannot see?
Are you so deaf that you cannot hear?
Are you so dumb that you cannot speak? I say

Free Nelson Mandela
Free Nelson Mandela
Free Nelson Mandela

The Special A.K.A., 1984[4]

The day before Mandela died, the *Cape Times* – Cape Town's morning newspaper – carried two short news stories separated by a photograph captioned 'Our Icon'. The first item reported that a photographic portrait of Nelson Mandela had been sold for a record $200,000. The portrait, by Adrian Stern, was sold to a New York private collector who wished to remain anonymous.

The second story reported the announcement in Johannesburg of a book in production – the *Nelson Mandela Opus*. The book would be half a metre square and weigh 37 kilograms. Only 10,000 copies would be available worldwide – although 'derivatives' would be more widely available. The book, in burnished leather covers, was being produced by Opus Media, self-badged as 'the foremost luxury publishing brand'. It was the latest title in a series on 'iconic organisations and personalities, which include brands such as Formula One, Ferrari, Manchester United, Michael Jackson, Sachin Tendulkar and the Springboks'.

This chapter is not about Mandela as a brand, or as a commodity; yet the pricey portrait and the brazen excesses of the Opus project cannot be comprehended without some sense of the construction, over several decades, of an iconic Mandela. In the years from 1950 to 1990 the person of Mandela became the vehicle for an increasing freight of symbolic meaning. Many hands were involved in the enterprise, adding details, heightening the lustre, positioning the heroic subject in ever more favourable light. But crucial contributions to the project, in the 1950s and early 1960s, were made by Mandela himself.

All the major commentators on Nelson Mandela have noted his acute awareness of his own presence, of the potency of the image and the strength of the symbolic gesture or stance. Elleke Boehmer writes of 'his chameleon-like talent for donning different disguises; his theatrical flair for costume and gesture; his shrewd awareness of the power of his own image'. Tom Lodge places special emphasis on 'Mandela's political actions as performance, self-consciously planned, scripted to meet public expectations, or calculated to shift popular sentiment … For Mandela, politics has always been primarily about enacting stories, about making narratives.'[5]

Richard Stengel, who worked closely with Mandela as editor and co-writer of the autobiography *Long Walk to Freedom*, presses the case even further. Throughout his life, Mandela was concerned with how things looked. He loved clothes: 'He always has … His view is that if you want to play the part, you have to wear the right costume.' And so as a young lawyer, Mandela wore bespoke suits to impress the court; when he went underground, he donned fatigues and grew a beard. Mandela was not merely sartorially sensitive, he was 'concerned about appearances on a far grander scale than just what suit he was wearing. He understood the power of the image ... Mandela thought deeply about how his actions would be interpreted by voters or the media ... "Appearances constitute reality", he once said to me.' As a young man, Mandela was keen to be photographed; as elder statesman, he loved the celebrity photo-op: 'Like Lincoln, who took every opportunity to have his picture taken, Mandela is aware that images have tremendous power.' 'All his life, he cultivated and curated images of himself.'[6]

As the young Mandela rose rapidly through the ranks of the African National Congress (ANC) in the 1950s, he emerged as one of its most visible and popular leaders. The novelist Lewis Nkosi recalls him during this decade: 'a tall, handsome man with hair parted in the middle ... wearing a charcoal grey suit and [flashing] a big white-toothed smile of success.' In her autobiography, *Call Me Woman*, Ellen Kuzwayo wrote: 'I remember the glamorous Nelson Mandela of those years. The beautiful white silk scarf he wore round his neck stands out in my mind to this day.'[7]

Mandela and his photogenic second wife, Winnie, often featured in the pages of *Drum* magazine (edited by Anthony Sampson, later Mandela's official biographer), radiating style, confidence and ambition. Tom Lodge reminds us that *Drum* carried 'the first photo-journalism directed at black readers', and in its pages Mandela became 'a visually public personality'.[8] Defining moments in Mandela's self-presentation took place after the crisis precipitated by the Sharpeville shootings in March 1960 and by the ANC's decision – after it was banned by the government – to operate illegally. By March 1961, Mandela was in hiding – yet not out of the spotlight.

On 22 March he made a surprise appearance at a conference in Pietermaritzburg, a show of strength for the proscribed ANC. Mandela was rapturously greeted by the 1,400 delegates: 'the panache of his emergence from hiding gave his image a new magic,' says Sampson.[9] Over the next couple of months, Mandela held a series of covert meetings with journalists, pressing the justice of his cause – and was dubbed the Black Pimpernel, a soubriquet whose appeal he cultivated. Mandela spent the first six months of 1962 visiting independent African states (and made a brief trip to London). He returned to South Africa – clandestinely – in July 1962, but was captured by the police two weeks later.

Mandela was taken aback during his African travels by the extent to which the rival Pan Africanist Congress (PAC) was seen by some African leaders as more authentically African: the ANC in their eyes was compromised by its alliance with whites, Indians and coloureds. Ever since the formation of the PAC, Mandela had countered its Africanist claims. In 1961, he arranged to have his photograph taken by Eli Weinberg in African 'tribal' dress as a visual reminder of his own 'authentic' identity. This produced the familiar image of a seated Mandela, torso bared, wearing a beaded necklace, bracelets and a blanket. The message was clear: here was a dignified, powerful African proud of his traditions and heritage.

Even more explicit was Mandela's dramatic stage management of his trial in Pretoria in October 1962. Charged with inciting a strike and with leaving the country illegally, he entered the courtroom wearing a traditional Xhosa *kaross* (a cape made of animal skin). Winnie attended, wearing Xhosa headwear and an ankle-length skirt. His costume expressed visually what Mandela told the court: 'this trial is a trial of the aspirations of the African people.' Years later, he spelled it out: 'I had chosen traditional dress to emphasize the symbolism that I was a black African walking into a white man's court.' [10]

The magistrate sentenced Mandela to five years' imprisonment, so he was already in prison when his senior ANC colleagues were arrested at Liliesleaf Farm in Rivonia, Johannesburg, in July 1963. Mandela joined the others as Accused No. 1 in what became known as the Rivonia Trial. From the dock, he made a speech which remains his best-known public utterance. After nearly three hours, Mandela concluded by putting down his papers and speaking from memory:

> I have cherished the ideal of a democratic and free society in which all persons live together in harmony and with equal opportunities. It is an ideal which I hope to live for, and see realized. But if needs be, it is an ideal for which I am prepared to die.

Mandela's speech – which outlined the ANC's history and the reasons for launching a sabotage campaign – and especially its remarkable peroration were widely reported at the time and quoted over and again in later years. It was the key text underpinning his iconic status as nationalist leader and as political prisoner.

If Mandela himself was a prime shaper of his image, as it took form, the most important agent in the longer term was the organisation which he came to symbolise: the African National Congress. Founded in 1912, it was for nearly forty years the vehicle of a tiny stratum of African intellectuals and professionals; in the 1950s it embraced the tactics of civil disobedience and recruited thousands of new members. In 1955, the ANC and its allies convened the Congress of the People and adopted the Freedom Charter – a ringing call for equal rights for all South Africans. Banned in 1960, the ANC's dual response was to set up a presence in exile and to operate illegally inside South Africa.

In early 1961 the internal ANC leaders, including Mandela, made the challenging shift to clandestine activism. Reflecting on the moment thirty-four years later, Walter Sisulu – Mandela's closest friend and comrade – said that he believed at the time that the ANC should have a single leader underground, and that it must be Mandela: 'When we decided that he should go underground I knew that he was now stepping into a position of leadership … We had got the leadership outside but we must have a leader in jail.' Anthony Sampson comments that Sisulu 'clearly foresaw the need for a martyr'.[11]

In October 1962, as Mandela awaited his first trial, the underground ANC distributed leaflets headed 'Mandela is in Prison: The People are in Chains', promoting 'the new image of Mandela as the uncompromising outlaw, the lone fighter who symbolised the unity of the people'.[12] Once the trial began, the ANC set up a Free Mandela Committee, issuing the call, 'Free Mandela'. In his autobiography, Mandela recalls that 'the slogan began to appear scrawled on the sides of buildings'.[13] Twenty years later, the call to 'Free Nelson Mandela' was daubed on countless walls again – but not only in South Africa. It became the rallying cry of an international solidarity movement, a pop song, a staple of editorials and headlines around the world, a demand and a credo.

It was not a call that echoed consistently from the early 1960s to the 1980s. A petition opposing death sentences for the Rivonia accused won 180,000 signatories; but after the verdict the campaign lost its *raison d'être* and its momentum. Global awareness of Mandela, which flared briefly in response to the Rivonia speech and his life sentence, subsided. The attention span of international media is limited. In 1964 the London *Times* referred to Mandela fifty-eight times, and the *New York Times* made twenty-four mentions. By the following year these figures had shrunk to two and none. For the next ten years, Mandela scarcely existed in the global consciousness: the icon was out of sight and largely out of mind. Even in the British Anti-Apartheid Movement (AAM), not a single action for Mandela was taken between 1967 and 1970.

The crucial phase in the making of Mandela as the symbol of the struggle against apartheid was the late

1970s and early 1980s. International awareness of South Africa was rekindled by the Soweto revolt of mid-1976 and by the death of Steve Biko in September 1977. The exiled ANC was a major beneficiary of the Soweto rising: several thousand militant youngsters left South Africa and joined the ANC and its guerrilla army, Umkhonto we Sizwe (MK), to continue their struggle against the white minority regime. In the UK, a group called South Africa: The Imprisoned Society (SATIS) was launched in 1974, focusing on political prisoners and operating under the auspices of the British AAM.

It was SATIS which proposed marking Mandela's sixtieth birthday, in July 1978, with a campaign to send him cards. The London office of the ANC approved the initiative, and the International Defence and Aid Fund marked the birthday by republishing a collection of Mandela's speeches and writings that had first appeared in 1965.[14] This sixtieth birthday campaign signalled a new focus on Mandela, and the AAM quickly realised that personifying the struggle made it easier to win support.

The headquarters of the exiled ANC was in Lusaka, Zambia. By the late 1970s, the organisation had created a new structure with various departments – for education, health, economics, and so on. Among these was a highly effective Department of Information and Publicity (DIP), whose staff included future ANC heavyweights Thabo Mbeki, Pallo Jordan and Joel Netshitenzhe. The DIP observed the impact of the sixtieth birthday campaign in the UK and followed suit; they decided to use anniversaries of significant 'struggle' dates and personalities as part of a strategy to humanise the fight against apartheid. In an internal memo the DIP recognised that 'the media will want to use names and individuals ... It is human interest that sells politics!'[15]

This marked a conscious departure by the ANC from its previous practice of only promoting a collective leadership and avoiding a focus on individuals. In March 1980, at the urging of the Lusaka leadership, Percy Qoboza, editor of the Johannesburg *Sunday Post*, launched a petition on the front page for Mandela's release. The headline read, 'Free Mandela'.

So a call first made in the early 1960s began to reverberate in the 1980s. The ANC had lit the touch-paper; but even its media-savvy DIP could not have anticipated how the rocket would take off. The British AAM had used Mandela's sixtieth birthday to launch its Free Nelson Mandela campaign, and in response to Qoboza's daring journalism, it redoubled its efforts. There ensued the biggest and most successful campaign the AAM ever undertook; it caught the imagination of people and organisations all over the world, triggering similar initiatives, and it was extremely well timed. Inside South Africa, the United Democratic Front (founded in August 1983) led internal resistance to unprecedented levels. President P.W. Botha's government eventually suppressed the protests, but so brutally that it lost any lingering shreds of legitimacy.

It was against this backdrop, playing out on television screens across the world, that the AAM's campaign gathered such remarkable momentum. A burgeoning international solidarity movement was the third crucial agent in the Mandela mythopoeia. But which Mandela – what kind of hero – did the campaign construct?

First, it portrayed a man of extraordinary personal qualities: intelligent, eloquent, principled, a natural leader. His virtues were universally legible: courage, honour and commitment to 'an ideal for which I am prepared to die'. His personal appeal was heightened by a romantic ideal alongside the political saga. His beautiful wife, also harassed by apartheid's police, was a powerful custodian of the icon. Mandela's turn to armed struggle (which remained contentious, as it had when Amnesty International decided it could not adopt him as a Prisoner of Conscience) was explained as a recourse adopted only when all other channels of peaceful protest had been blocked.

Second, the campaign presented Mandela as symbol, as synecdoche. Mandela stood for the ANC: he personified its resilience, its non-racialism, its leadership of the liberation movement. Mandela represented all South African political prisoners, regardless of political affiliation. Even more expansively, he exemplified 'the courage and determination of the black people of South Africa to overthrow apartheid'.[16]

Third, by the mid-1980s, Mandela was depicted increasingly as leader-in-waiting, as indispensable to his country's future. In South Africa and internationally, the campaign conveyed an 'avowedly reverential, redemptive version of Mandela's political and ethical significance'. In effect, this rhetoric echoed Oliver Tambo's daring 1978 claim that Mandela was 'in the front ranks of the authentic leadership of the people of South Africa and a respected world statesman'.[17]

From 1985, Mandela was visited in Pollsmoor prison by various dignitaries, and their slightly awestruck accounts added gloss to the legend. A wide-eyed American academic wrote of his encounter: 'I felt that I was in the presence not of a guerrilla fighter or radical ideologue, but of a head of state.' A British peer said he was welcomed by a tall, self-assured man who 'shook my hand and greeted me in precise educated English' and that, after two hours together, he 'felt poorer at being so suddenly deprived of the man's exhilarating company'. In 1986, members of a Commonwealth Eminent Persons group were 'struck by his immaculate appearance … and his commanding presence'. (The appearance was no accident: Mandela wrote with some satisfaction of being measured by a tailor for a 'pin-striped suit that fitted me like a glove … The [prison] commander admired my new attire. "Mandela, you look like a prime minister now, not a prisoner", he said and smiled.')[18]

He was not yet head of state, but honoured as if he were: countless streets and buildings were named for Mandela and he was garlanded with honours and awards. The AAM campaign entered mainstream politics. When the South African embassy in London refused to accept a birthday card for Mandela in 1978, British Prime Minister James Callaghan sent greetings from the floor of the House of

Commons. In 1982, Michael Foot and David Steel, leaders of the Labour and Liberal parties, formally called for Mandela's release. By 1985 Margaret Thatcher, in a rare concession to public opinion, added her voice to the call for his release – all the more striking given her earlier hostility to the ANC and refusal to become involved in the campaign.

The campaign peaked in mid-1988, to mark the iconic absentee's seventieth birthday. There were rallies and marches. The centrepiece was a pop concert at Wembley. A capacity audience sang along and danced as a line-up of headline artists performed for ten hours. The BBC broadcast the event live, making it available to stations worldwide. The global audience in sixty-three countries was estimated at 500 million. Half a billion people watched a highly politicised piece of popular culture. Half a billion people heard one entertainer after the other call for the overthrow of apartheid and for the release of its famous opponent. 'The concert raised the stakes by universalising Mandela's significance. "Until you are free", Stevie Wonder told Mandela, "no man or woman or child of any culture or colour is free."'[19] An icon long in the making now became transcendent. Mandela, the man, was everyman. Mandela, the prisoner, was prophet, liberator, a hero poised for return: he was Moses, Bolivar, Ulysses.

It is relatively easy to trace the history of Mandela's status as living legend. It is virtually impossible to imagine what it must have been like to inhabit such space, to live as individual and as legend – particularly for an intensely private, self-disciplined man to be the focus of such public adulation. Mandela was keenly aware of being made the symbol of the struggle. In prison he kept a record of correspondence, visits, news and the like with entries on a series of desk calendars. From 10 October 1980 onwards (when he noted, '73,000 people sign petition for the release of N.M.'), the entries included a log of external support: the Nehru Award, nomination as Chancellor of London University, a call for release by the UN Committee Against Apartheid, Archbishop Desmond Tutu addressing MPs at the culmination of the Release Mandela campaign, honorary degrees, erection of plaques and statues – and so on.[20]

Verne Harris of the Mandela Foundation's Centre of Memory worked closely with him in his later years, arranging and classifying his archives. Mandela, he says, felt an 'enormous burden of responsibility' when the ANC chose to personify the liberation struggle around him. Frequently, in letters from prison and in conversations with visitors, he stressed that he was only human. Wryly, he told a visitor in the late 1980s, 'I am not a God or a prophet but I have to act like one.' Just six months before his release, he told Fatima Meer – an old friend and early biographer – that he was worried by how much was expected of him: 'if all these super-expectations can be overcome, I can work nicely.' Mandela was sensitive to the potency of his image, his symbolic capital: 'He was also aware that you pay a price:

the human being that you are starts to lose connection with that public representation.'[21]

That loss of connection between self and image was poignantly manifested at Adelaide Tambo's funeral in 2007. When Mandela left the event he was recognised: his car was thronged by well-wishers, shouting and waving. The old man turned to his aide, Vimla Naidoo, bewildered and uncertain: 'How do they know who I am?' he asked. The irony was profound, and tragic. Perhaps the best-known person on the planet had momentarily forgotten who he was – or, more accurately, had forgotten who his public persona was. The man had slipped his moorings from the icon.

2

Early Years: The Making of a Nationalist

Though you were of a minor house, the iXhiba
Jongintaba picked you

Brought you to the Royal Home
To the house of No-Inglani, his wife
The woman with the long breast, daughter of Krune,
To the Royal Home, fount of the culture
And custom of a people
The Royal Home where the art of service
To the nations is learnt.

Nogqaza we Jojo, 1989[22]

Nelson Mandela was 12 years old when he left his home, a straggling village of a hundred huts scattered over a grassy valley cupped between hills. His father had just died. After a few days of mourning, his mother told him that he was to leave Qunu – although not where he was bound, nor why. In an unusually emotional passage of his autobiography, Mandela recalled walking westwards, behind his mother: 'I mourned less for my father than for the world I was leaving behind. Qunu was all that I knew, and I loved it in the unconditional way that a child loves his first home.' [23]

Three-quarters of a century later, Mandela built a home in Qunu. Initially, he used it to snatch weekends away from politics; in his retirement, he divided his time between Qunu and Johannesburg. In Qunu, he designated the spot where he wished to be buried; and it was there that he was eventually laid to rest. His unfeigned affection for the rural Transkei is telling; it reflects his view of himself. In the sequel to his autobiography he stressed that he 'grew up in a country village until I was twenty-three' (when he first saw city life), 'But … my opinions were already formed from the countryside'.[24]

What kind of rural society shaped the young Mandela? The Transkei was a product of colonial rule but a region in which precolonial dynamics and structures also persisted. The Transkeian Territories comprised a bloc the size of Switzerland between the nineteenth-century British colonies of the Cape and Natal. By 1894, the entire territory had been incorporated into the Cape Colony and its component parts and peoples – including Gcaleka, Mfengu, Mpondomise, Mpondo and Thembu – began to be viewed as a unit.

The Transkei was made up of twenty-six districts, each under the sway of a magistrate reporting to a chief magistrate in Umtata. Before 1910, the Transkei was administered separately from the Cape Colony proper, under a form of indirect rule. Once the Union of South Africa was formed in 1910, the Transkei became the largest 'native reserve' in the country: an area set aside specifically to house large numbers of Africans. Just over 1 million Africans lived in the Transkei at the time of Union.

In the precolonial era, Xhosa-speaking peoples lived in this region, in groupings of various sizes; political power in each was wielded by a hierarchy of hereditary chiefs and counsellors. By the time Mandela was born, the chiefs had lost much of their power. The system of indirect rule meant that chiefs and headmen served as agents of the local magistrate, helping him collect taxes, maintain law and order (in a remarkably peaceful society) and implementing a thicket of regulations governing the movement of people and livestock.

Crucially, the precolonial chieftaincies survived. Although they were enmeshed in the new administrative system, they continued to wield older powers. Chiefs conducted court hearings in what was recognised as 'customary law'; they collected tributary fees and dues from their followers; they oversaw the distribution of land. More than this, they were custodians of custom and continuity. For many of their traditionalist followers, the authority and prestige of the chiefs was preferable to that of the whites: magistrates, missionaries, traders and labour recruiters.

Indirect rule imposed the presence of the South African state in the Transkei but blunted its impact. For most Transkeians, the physical and social environment remained broadly intact. They held to beliefs, rituals, culture and identities that were essentially precolonial. Relations between commoners and chiefs, between men and women, and between children and adults were still regulated by conventions and customs that predated the colonial presence. There were strong forces of change at work in the region: conversion to Christianity and school attendance generated a new elite stratum, while tax obligations and the lure of trade goods led more and more young men into migrant labour, leaving the Transkei to earn wages. Yet people clung tenaciously to their rural identities; most families retained access to land, their lives patterned by the rhythms of sowing and harvest, and care of flocks and herds.

The macro- and micro-politics of indirect rule, and the tug of war between change and continuity, bore directly on Mandela's life. He was born into a junior line of the

Thembu royalty: his father was a local headman. But the journey he made at the age of 12 took him to the epicentre of Thembu power. His mother led him to Mqhekezweni, the Great Place or court of Chief Jongintaba. The heir to the Thembu paramount chieftainship was a young boy, and Jongintaba was acting as regent. He had promised Mandela's ailing father, Mphakanyiswa Mandela, that he would be guardian to his youngest son. He honoured this commitment, and Mandela grew up as a ward in the royal household, treated as a member of the family.

Mandela was born on 18 July 1918 and was named Rolihlahla ('he who shakes the branch of a tree'). His father was headman at Mvezo, where Mandela was born, and in this capacity also a counsellor to the paramount chief. He was every inch a traditionalist: illiterate, a polygamist, and he never converted to Christianity. Each of his four wives established her own homestead, and these were several miles apart. Rolihlahla's mother, Nosekeni, moved with him to Qunu in his infancy.

Nosekeni took the Christian name Fanny when she joined the local Wesleyan church, and she baptised her son as a Methodist. Church membership and schooling came as part of a package, and when Mandela was 7, Fanny sent him to the one-roomed primary school at Qunu. On his first day at school the teacher gave each of her new pupils an English or 'school name'. Rolihlahla became Nelson. (When he underwent circumcision – a Xhosa ritual signifying adulthood – he took the additional name

Dalibhunga. In later life, Mandela was addressed by those close to him as Madiba, a clan honorific, and increasingly it was as Madiba that he was familiarly and affectionately known by South Africans.)

The boy's move to Mqhekezweni emphasised elements of his identity. A headman's son, he was now the regent's ward; baptised as a Methodist, he was now in a household where 'religion was part of the fabric of life'; having taken his first steps towards literacy in Qunu, he was now required by his guardian to be 'properly' educated. Nelson Rolihlahla was 16 years old when Jongintaba drove him to the century-old Wesleyan boarding school, Clarkebury, the pinnacle of education for Africans in Thembuland.

Here, Mandela passed the Junior Certificate in two rather than the normal three years. A highly retentive memory, much commented on during his later years, was first apparent at Clarkebury. The next step in his educational journey took Mandela to Healdtown in the Eastern Cape in 1937. The school housed over 800 pupils and it offered the Senior Certificate, the highest grade of schooling available in South Africa. Only half a dozen mission schools in the country provided this opportunity to African students.

From Healdtown, with his Senior Certificate, in 1939 Mandela proceeded to Fort Hare. Founded in 1916, Fort Hare was the only institution of higher education for black students in South Africa. There were only 200 students on the tiny campus when Mandela registered for a BA, taking courses in law, native administration, politics and English.

In his second year, however, before he completed the degree, he refused to back down from a confrontation with the principal, Dr Kerr, and was expelled.

Mandela returned to the Great Place, and to the displeasure of Jongintaba. Displeasure soon became fury. Jongintaba had identified two women whom he wished Mandela and his own son, Justice, to marry. The young men recoiled from the arranged marriages, fled the Great Place and travelled to Johannesburg. The regent was livid at their disobedience and betrayal. He had groomed Justice and Nelson for life as Thembu chief and counsellor, but ironically his investment in their education had widened their horizons and provoked change rather than the continuity he desired.

Mandela was 23 years old when he went to Johannesburg, by his own account a country bumpkin, utterly unprepared for life in the big city. Unprepared, perhaps; but not without resources. First, Mandela entered adulthood as a member of two overlapping elites: the Thembu aristocracy and the upper reaches of a highly educated meritocracy. His self-confidence was rooted in esteem accrued in the Great Place and the classroom. Second, his intelligence and education opened doors for him in Johannesburg that were closed to most Africans. Within months, Mandela was working as a clerk in a legal firm and was bent upon becoming a lawyer.

Africans called Johannesburg eGoli, and city of gold it was. It existed because of the discovery in 1886 of the world's richest deposits of the precious metal. It began as an unruly mining camp and by the 1940s had mushroomed into a highly segregated city of over 800,000 people. There were older enclaves of black settlement in Alexandra and Sophiatown, but increasingly Africans were concentrated in townships south-west of the city, in the drably uniform 'matchbox' houses of Soweto.

Mandela spent most of the 1940s and all of the 1950s in the city, a pivotal era for its black population. The African townships swirled with culture and creativity; they were vibrant and violent, punctuated by episodes of political protest and mobilisation. American influences permeated township jazz, township gangs and township journalism, inviting comparison with the Harlem Renaissance of the 1920s.

The townships were crucibles of change, especially during the Second World War. Goods previously imported were now made in the country; black workers filled jobs vacated by nearly 200,000 white men in uniform; average wages rose; and migrants poured into the cities. Johannesburg's black population nearly doubled, to more than 400,000. Crucially, more women were moving to and staying in urban areas: a black working class permanently separated from the land became a new social reality.

It was a population chafing at cost-of-living issues, the shortage of housing and the plethora of controls over movement and rights to residence. From 1943 to 1946, in this urban cauldron, protests and grassroots resistance simmered and sometimes boiled over. There were anti-pass campaigns, bus boycotts, wildcat walk-outs and a momentous strike by African miners in 1946. There were waves of squatter movements, when landless people threw up shanty towns on unoccupied land.

These tensions and flashpoints elicited two powerful political reactions: a more vigorous form of African nationalism on the one hand, and a drive to political power by Afrikaner nationalists under the banner of apartheid on the other.

Within the ANC, a group of younger men formed an ANC Youth League (YL), launched in April 1944. The Youth Leaguers criticised their elders as 'a body of gentlemen with clean hands', lacking ambition and clear goals. To address these shortcomings, the YL promised to become 'the brains-trust and power-station' of African nationalism. By 1949, the YL delivered: the parent body adopted the YL's Programme of Action at its annual conference. The programme committed the ANC to employ boycotts, strikes and civil disobedience to achieve 'national freedom' and 'self-determination'.[25]

The resurgence of Afrikaner nationalism was evident in the surprise victory in the 1948 general election for the National Party (NP), which had promised to halt African urbanisation, protect white workers against competition from black workers, provide white farmers with black labour and generally to tighten existing segregation. A major plank in its electoral platform was a relatively new slogan: apartheid (separateness), promising rigorous racial segregation to white voters long accustomed to beliefs and behaviour premised on racial difference.

It was in these currents – a distinctive township culture, black working-class protests, the galvanic impact of the YL on the ANC, and a lurch to the right by white voters in 1948 – that the young Mandela navigated, with some aplomb. Johannesburg was absolutely crucial in shaping Mandela personally, politically and professionally.

In his personal life, Mandela was upwardly mobile, socially active and increasingly at home in the city. Early concerns about what to wear to a party, and embarrassment at wearing a second-hand suit (given to him by an employer) to work soon eased. Social anxieties and financial pressures receded as he settled into the job at the law firm. He began to earn a reputation as a snappy dresser and 'man about town'. He indulged his love of music and dancing; he was a keen boxer, sparring for ninety minutes whenever he could and running in the early mornings.

Shortly after arriving in Johannesburg, he met Walter Sisulu. There commenced the closest and most influential friendship Mandela ever made. Sisulu was six years older. Although he had only been educated as far as the first year of secondary school, he radiated a city-smart intelligence and came to have a profound effect on Mandela's politics. Sisulu brokered Mandela's legal job; and it was at his home that Mandela met Evelyn Mase, a young nurse. The two fell for each other and married in 1944. In 1947, they moved to a three-roomed house in Orlando West, an enclave of better-off Africans.

The couple had two sons and a daughter. Mandela took an active part in bringing up the children: bathing and feeding the babies, telling them stories before sleep, shopping and occasionally cooking. Yet, as he acknowledged, the pleasures of domesticity were rationed: 'I was rarely at home to enjoy such things.' The marriage came under increasing strain and collapsed some time before its formal conclusion in divorce.

Politically, Mandela's beliefs and allegiances grew directly from urban life. He had never heard of the ANC before he went to Fort Hare and took scant notice of it even there. The young man who fled to the city from an arranged marriage was effectively without political views. Life in Johannesburg soon changed that. Political realities were inescapable. White authority and wealth were juxtaposed with black poverty and rightlessness. This basic lesson was dramatised by countless petty slights of institutionalised racism; it was brutally scripted in the passbook that urban African men were required to carry at all times.

In August 1943 the people of Alexandra township mounted a successful bus boycott in protest against a fare increase; for ten days, thousands walked 6 miles in and 6 miles out until the company restored the 4-penny fare. An organiser of the protest was Gaur Radebe, the only other African working at the law firm where Mandela was employed, an ANC and Communist Party activist. Mandela joined Radebe and marched with the boycotters. It was, he wrote later, the moment he crossed the line from being an observer to becoming a participant.

He began attending ANC meetings; and in September 1943 he met Anton Lembede at Sisulu's home. Lembede was a brilliant, puritanical firebrand, South Africa's Robespierre. He died in 1947, aged just 33, but in 1943 had been the intellectual leader of the group of young men – including Mandela and Sisulu – who lobbied for the creation of a Youth League within the ANC. When the YL was formed in April 1944, Mandela was elected to its executive. His initial, tentative excursions into African nationalism had become more insistent, more committed.

Between 1944 and 1949, Mandela's political position was modelled on Lembede: he was 'hostile to all suggestion of collaboration with white, Indian or communist groups'.[26] Like Lembede, Mandela insisted on African control and leadership as prerequisites to African liberation. This represented the 'Africanist' strain within the ANC, in tension for over a decade with a 'nationalist' strain more amenable to strategic alliances and non-racialism. Mandela's political journey began in the former camp, but by the late 1940s it had begun to shift to the latter.

As an Africanist, Mandela was notably hostile to the Indian Congresses; but when Indians sustained a passive resistance campaign against a law preventing them from buying land, Mandela was struck by their solidarity. As a Lembede disciple, Mandela was strongly opposed to the influence of the Communist Party on the ANC. Yet at the same time he admired the role of communists in helping organise the 1946 miners' strike, and from the outset he was struck by the non-racialism of the communists he met. Mandela's Africanism became increasingly at odds with the composition of his circle of friends beyond

Orlando. He grew close to Indian and white communists such as Ismail Meer, Yusuf Cachalia and Amina Pahad, Ruth First and Michael Harmel. In theory and practice, Mandela shifted from Africanist orthodoxy towards multi-racial comradeship.

Mandela did not attend the ANC's December 1949 conference, but was associated with the YL's success when the parent body approved its Programme of Action and replaced Dr Xuma with Dr James Moroka as president. Sisulu was elected secretary-general, and in 1950 he nominated Mandela to fill a vacancy on the National Executive Committee of the ANC.

Professionally, Mandela began his legal apprenticeship as an articled clerk in 1943. Having completed his BA by correspondence, he enrolled at the University of the Witwatersrand (Wits) for a law degree, attending classes from 1943 to 1949. His standing, confidence and income were assured. Mandela was in a middle-class job, and his salary rose as he gained experience. At Wits, Ismail Meer later recalled, Mandela was 'the best-dressed student' in their circle. Invited by Meer to a clothing sale in down-market Vrededorp, Mandela 'looked down his nose and said, "I shop at Markhams."'[27] A couple of years later he was having his suits handmade by the tailor who dressed the millionaire Harry Oppenheimer.

By 1950 it was clear that Mandela would not complete his Wits law degree. Instead, he sat the Attorneys' Admission Examination and was admitted as an attorney. As Phil Bonner puts it, Mandela used his new affluence 'to adopt the style of a township big shot. He bought a huge Oldsmobile sedan ... He cavorted with countless beautiful women.'[28] In 1952 Mandela set up his own practice, joined later that year by Oliver Tambo. It was a landmark year. The pair became partners in a pioneering African-owned legal office that developed into a highly profitable practice until the Treason Trial began in 1957.

In 1950, the Thembu aristocrat was still discernible. The tall, well-dressed young man in his early thirties, aware of his own imposing presence, was given to flashes of anger and impetuosity. This is the Mandela evoked by Oliver Tambo years later: 'passionate, emotional, sensitive, quickly stung to bitterness and retaliation by insult and patronage.'[29]

But a different persona was also present. This was the political activist, neglecting law degree and family, willing to serve as 'heckler and disrupter-in-chief' at meetings of the rival Communist Party; an interventionist rather than a strategist. He developed a reputation, he later conceded, as 'a gadfly': he knew what he was against but was less clear as to what he was for and how to achieve it. In *Long Walk to Freedom* Mandela neatly captured the blend of commitment and callowness of his Youth League years: by 1955, after the Congress of the People, 'I had reached the light heavyweight division and carried more pounds and more responsibility', but in 1948 'I was an untested lightweight in the ANC.'[30]

3

Defiance and Rivonia: The Training of a Heavyweight

The child is not dead
Not at Langa nor at Nyanga
nor at Orlando nor at
Sharpeville
nor at the police post at Philippi
where he lies with a bullet
through his brain...

The child who became a giant travels through the
whole world
Without a pass

From 'The Child is not Dead' by Ingrid Jonker*

*This poem, originally written in Afrikaans, in response
to the Sharpeville shooting in March 1960 was read by
Nelson Mandela in his inaugural address to Parliament in
May 1994.

The National Party (NP) government, elected in 1948 on the promise of apartheid, remained in power until 1994. Apartheid welded racial discrimination into law, created an Orwellian system of control and repression and required ever more authoritarian means to uphold it. In the 1950s, the NP enacted the core elements of apartheid, making racial separation more systematic and rigorous. As Minister of Native (later Bantu) Affairs, H.F. Verwoerd extended state control over African education, housing and access to the cities. Political control of the state was exclusively for whites. For Africans, Verwoerd devised an elaborate system of limited local government in the rural 'reserves': it was pointless, said Verwoerd, for 'the Bantu' to engage in 'general principles of higher politics'.[31]

Apartheid can be described by listing its legislation and recounting the relentless bureaucratic application of these laws. It is far more difficult to convey the lived experience of apartheid: what it meant to be on the wrong side of the colour line in a system where racial classification defined one's identity, one's rights and the conditions of daily being. For Africans in the apartheid era, the sociologist Deborah Posel remarks, 'all the minutiae of everyday life – where and with whom they lived, had sex, travelled, shopped, walked or sat down, what they owned and consumed' were governed by passes, permits and prohibitions.[32] For black South Africans, ordinary urban life was criminalised: at their peak, the Pass Laws jailed millions of Africans per decade for being in the wrong place at the wrong time, without the right papers. And, in addition to the formal proscriptions of apartheid laws, there was a constant unthinking and informal racism. South Africa was a segregated society before apartheid; under apartheid, racial discrimination was inscribed in law and also experienced in countless routine encounters.

Throughout the decade the state expanded its coercive powers and shredded civil liberties. The NP's determination to snuff out organised black resistance saw government and its opponents in hostile lockstep. The Defiance Campaign of 1952 triggered swingeing penalties and new clampdowns on public gatherings. The Congress of the People in 1955 begat the Treason Trial. In 1960, an anti-pass demonstration was met by the Sharpeville massacre and the banning of the two main African nationalist movements. By mid-1961, the PAC and the ANC had both opted for violent forms of struggle.

Nelson Mandela was directly involved in this dynamic of intensified confrontation and repression. He became increasingly prominent within the ANC, elected successively to executive positions in the YL, the Transvaal ANC and the national body. Several factors were at play. He had Sisulu's constant backing and tutelage, and he was seen as a Youth Leaguer responsible for a new leadership and new strategy within the ANC. He was also admired for personal attributes: intense commitment, an ability to persuade and a confidence that could be 'regal and maybe a bit distant', as Albertina Sisulu put it years later.[33] He became a highly visible professional and activist, with a flair for being seen and a taste for the limelight.

His heightened political profile by 1952 was largely due, the historian Philip Bonner has argued, to his ideological volte-face in 1951.[34] Mandela finally jettisoned his Africanist exclusivity and became an advocate of multi-racial alliance politics. He also moved leftwards, becoming ideologically closer to members of the South African Communist Party (SACP), as well as cementing friendships.[35] There may have been a dash of apostate ardence in the warmth of his embrace of the Defiance Campaign as a joint action between the ANC and its allies: Indians, coloureds and whites in separate congresses. Yet, once the ANC appointed Mandela as volunteer-in-chief of the campaign, he was never going to be anything but wholehearted.

Launched in June 1952, the Defiance Campaign called for the repeal of six 'unjust' laws. It was a pageant of civil disobedience: groups of volunteers courted arrest by ignoring curfews, refusing to carry permits and entering 'whites only' public spaces. Over 8,000 volunteers were arrested, three-quarters of them in Port Elizabeth and East London. When popular anger flared in these Eastern Cape cities in November 1952 – with riots, violence and vicious police reprisals – the campaign petered out before being called off. Mandela's role was that of advising, recruiting and encouraging regional branches of the ANC, involving travel to Durban, Port Elizabeth and Cape Town.

For his efforts, he was one of nineteen leaders of the campaign put on trial in November 1952. They were found guilty under the sweeping Suppression of Communism Act (although, as the judge observed, 'This has nothing to do with communism as it is commonly known'). They were sentenced to nine months in prison, the penalty suspended. A week later Mandela was served with a banning order which proscribed his attending any meeting, speaking to more than one person at a time or leaving Johannesburg. It meant that henceforth all his 'actions and plans ... would become secret and illegal' and his political role 'peripheral'.[36]

While the Defiance Campaign failed to deflect the government from its aggressive policies, it was a victory of sorts. The ANC recruited 100,000 new members, winning a broad-based membership for the first time in its history. The campaign was the movement's high-water mark, the most successful protest mounted during the 1950s. In June 1955, the ANC and its allies convened a Congress of the People which adopted the Freedom Charter. Its resonant call for a non-racial society based on equality and social justice became important in the long term as the basic ANC policy statement, but at the time seemed only to give the state another stick with which to beat the ANC.

In December 1956 police arrested 156 members of the ANC and the allied congresses, and charged them with treason. Mandela, unsurprisingly, was among them. The prosecution alleged 'a countrywide conspiracy to use violence to overthrow the present government and replace it with a communist state', and the Freedom Charter was identified as key evidence of such intent. The case commenced in January 1957 and dragged on in various phases until March 1961. By then, only twenty-eight of those originally arrested still stood trial. Mandela was one of them. On 29 March 1961, the three presiding judges ruled that the state had failed to prove its case – and the remaining accused were discharged.

The trial drastically reduced the ability of the leadership to interact with the members of their organisations. The ANC mounted no significant campaigns during the late 1950s. The energies of its leaders were also taxed by the hostility to the Freedom Charter and its multi-racial principles which emanated from a group of Africanists; this was the group who broke away from the ANC in April 1959 to form the rival Pan Africanist Congress (PAC).

The Treason Trial had an impact on Mandela in other ways. The Mandela–Tambo law firm was profitable until both partners became entangled in the trial. Case-work had involved handling the affairs of Johannesburg's black elite; there had also been a steady flow of clients seeking legal protection from the pressures of apartheid. Mandela had developed something of a reputation for his court appearances, combining scrupulous observance of legal protocols and 'an assertive, theatrical style with sweeping gestures'.[37] Tambo, discharged as an accused in December

1957, did his best to sustain a limping practice, but it never recovered. By 1958, Mandela was in financial difficulties and in arrears on payments for a plot of land in the Transkei; he had no savings, not even a bank account.

The trial also put an end to his marriage to Evelyn. She was resentful and apprehensive about his activism; he disliked her fervent religiosity. Mandela spent more and more time away, and there were other women in his life. In 1957 he filed for divorce; by then he had met Winnie Nomzamo Madikizela. She had lived in Johannesburg for four years, and had recently qualified as a medical social worker. Winnie (Mandela called her Zami; she addressed him as Madiba) was just 22, fashion conscious, glamorous and uninvolved in politics. She was eighteen years younger than the high-profile lawyer who was captivated by her. It was an unusual courtship: Mandela juggled his time between court appearances and his own legal practice to be with Winnie as much as possible. He introduced her to his political confidants – 'I was both courting her and politicising her,' he later said[38] – and they accepted her because Mandela was so obviously smitten.

They married in June 1958, in Bizana in the Transkei, Winnie's home. The couple lived together as man and wife for only two years before Nelson left home to work underground. Even for those two years they lived in the shadow of the Treason Trial; time together competed with meetings, and home life was complicated by the presence of three alienated step-children and by the birth of a daughter, Zenani, in February 1959. Later, on Robben

Island, Mandela fed voraciously on memories of these two years. His letters to Winnie throb with retrospective intensity: he repeatedly recounted episodes of their life together, constructing, says Lodge, an 'idyllic domestic haven centred on her'.[39]

Winnie's recollections are different. In tones ranging from acceptance to irony to frustration, she reflected on the difficulties of those years. She discovered 'only too soon how quickly I would lose my identity ... with no name and no individuality except Mandela's'. In 1985 she wrote that Mandela 'did not even pretend that I would have some special claim to his time ... There never was any kind of life I can recall as family life ... the struggle, the nation came first.' She recalled the night he left their home, for the last time, without any notice: 'I quietly packed his clothes. I was in tears but I had been conditioned ... not to ask any questions.'[40]

The PAC, launched in 1959, was hostile to the ANC and to multi-racial politics. In all probability the racialised anger of the PAC more closely reflected popular discontent than the pronouncements of the ANC, which in any case were muffled by bannings and the Treason Trial. Rattled by the PAC's radical rhetoric, the ANC made a bid to regain ground. It announced an anti-pass campaign, due to begin on 31 March 1960, which would culminate in a bonfire of passes on 26 June. However, the PAC hit back and quickly approved its own, more militant, opposition to passes: on 18 March, despite scant preparation, it announced that its anti-pass campaign would begin just three days later.

On 21 March 1960 some 5,000 protestors gathered outside the police station at Sharpeville, near the steel-making town of Vereeniging. Panicky policemen opened fire, killing sixty-nine people. There ensued weeks of high drama, including an assassination attempt on the prime minister, Verwoerd. It seemed, briefly, that the NP's caretaker leadership might abandon the Pass Laws, but the security reflex over-ruled any reform possibilities. A State of Emergency was declared, and nearly 2,000 activists were arrested, including Mandela. Legislation was rushed through parliament declaring the ANC and PAC prohibited organisations.

Detentions under the State of Emergency lasted until the end of August. By then, Mandela's political persona had become somewhat schizophrenic. On the one hand, his evidence in the Treason Trial (he went to court each day, re-entering detention in the evening) provided an unambiguous statement of his own and the ANC's commitment to non-violence. On the other hand, throughout the later months of 1960, Mandela was a member of a group of ANC and SACP seniors moving to jettison non-violence as a principle and embrace instead a resort to armed struggle.

Elements within both the ANC and SACP were convinced well before Sharpeville that non-violence had run its course, especially in the Eastern Cape. In Johannesburg, Mandela and Sisulu had privately been discussing the possibility of armed struggle for years. Literature on guerrilla struggles in China, Vietnam and

Cuba circulated among the left and was studied intently. Such predilections appeared to be confirmed by outbreaks of rural protest from 1958 onwards: in Natal, in Zeerust, in Sekhukhuneland and in Pondoland popular struggles against the state used violent methods – and called (unavailingly) on the ANC for weapons.

In short, the turn to armed struggle was hastened, but not caused, by Sharpeville. Recourse to arms did not arise from a single, clear decision. It was a tumbleweed turning upon itself, buffeted by circumstances, gathering momentum, rolling towards resolution. Recent research has focused on a sequence of secret meetings and decisions in 1960 and 1961. It was at an SACP meeting in December 1960 that a formal resolution in favour of armed struggle was first taken. The ANC followed suit in June 1961.

A related issue, hotly debated in recent years, is whether Mandela had secretly joined the Communist Party by 1960. If he had, he would have joined Moses Kotane, J.B. Marks, Walter Sisulu and others as senior ANC figures who were also party members. Stephen Ellis and other scholars have insisted that Mandela became a member 'most likely in the late 1950s or in 1960 and that he was co-opted to the Central Committee in the latter year'. For Ellis, this meant that Mandela was one of a small group of communists who took the crucial decision in favour of arms and then manipulated the ANC into endorsing it six months later.[41]

The evidence for Mandela's membership is of the 'he said, she said' kind: statements by members of the party decades after the events in question. After Mandela's death, the SACP issued a statement claiming that when he was arrested in 1962, Mandela was a member of the party and its Central Committee. Yet, other members of the party have insisted that he never joined; Mandela himself went to some lengths to deny membership. He did so on trial: having admitted that he co-founded and led Umkhonto we Sizwe (MK – the ANC's armed wing and in exile its guerrilla army), membership of the SACP could hardly have affected his sentence. He denied it again, in 1967, in a letter to the Department of Justice, insisting that he had never been 'an office-bearer, officer, member or active supporter' of the party.

Perhaps the most convincing answer to the conundrum is given by Bob Hepple and the archivist Verne Harris. (Hepple was a member of the underground party; he was also Mandela's lawyer in his 1962 trial.) They agree that Mandela was at the crucial party meeting in December 1960, but that he attended as an invited observer, and that he was never committed to the party's aim of a socialist society. 'He was, and remained, an African nationalist.' It is, writes Hepple, 'entirely credible that Mandela was then co-opted onto the central committee to work closely with Joe Slovo, Walter Sisulu and others in establishing Umkhonto we Sizwe'.[42] Co-opted to work closely with communists, but not a member: this account explains why some communists later believed that Mandela had been a member, and why Mandela so strenuously denied it.

The MK leadership decided to carry out sabotage attacks on selected targets which were designed to avoid casualties. Leadership of MK was vested in a national high command, headed by Mandela and Slovo, with regional commands in Johannesburg, Durban, Port Elizabeth and Cape Town. By 16 December 1961, when the first explosions took place and the existence of MK was announced, there were about 250 recruits, organised in units of three to five members. These combatants were high on courage, commitment and bravado, but desperately short of training, relevant skills and appropriate materiel.

By December 1961, Mandela had been operating underground for nine months, living in a series of safe houses. The last of these was Liliesleaf Farm in the suburb of Rivonia. The SACP had bought the farm to hide 'people on the run'. From being a well-secured safe house, the farm now became the headquarters of MK. Mandela took no direct part in the sabotage attacks and, just days after they began, the ANC agreed that he should leave the country, attend an important meeting of newly independent African countries, and seek to win their political and material support for armed struggle.

Mandela left Johannesburg in January 1962 to spend six months travelling: from Dar-es-Salaam to Lagos and Addis Ababa, where he addressed a Pan-African Freedom Movement conference. Tunisia and Morocco followed; and next a swing through West Africa. Mandela then flew to London, meeting exiled activists but also British journalists and politicians, before returning to

Ethiopia. There is a tendency in the ANC's literature to see Mandela's brief exposure to military training and tactics by Algerian and Ethiopian soldiers as an index of revolutionary preparedness; in reality it had no practical outcome whatsoever.

Mandela returned to Liliesleaf on 24 July – dressed in military fatigues. After a brief reunion with Winnie, he reported on his travels to ANC and MK seniors. Two days later, brushing aside concerns about the safety of his trip, Mandela left for Natal. (Kathrada failed to get Mandela to shave his Guevarist beard, noting wryly years later that Nelson 'must have known how the beard enhanced his looks and personality'.) In Natal, he met Luthuli, ANC members and the MK regional command; he warned them that if sabotage did not effect change, 'we would probably move to guerrilla warfare'.[43] On the last night of the trip he attended a Congress party, again in his military khakis. The next day, 5 August, he set out to drive back to Johannesburg with Cecil Williams, a member of the Congress of Democrats. Their car was stopped. Both men were arrested.

In October 1962, Mandela stood trial in Pretoria, charged with incitement and with leaving the country illegally. With a guilty verdict the only possible outcome, Mandela opted for drama rather than legalism. He attended court in Xhosa regalia and he conducted his own defence. Before entering a plea, he challenged the court's right to hear his case: 'I consider myself neither legally nor morally bound to obey laws made by a parliament in which I have no representation.' The state called sixty witnesses; Mandela called none. His defence case consisted of a single sentence: 'Your Worship, I submit that I am guilty of no crimes.' A week later the case closed with his plea for mitigation – hardly a plea, rather an eloquent and defiant political manifesto.

Mandela denounced apartheid laws as 'immoral, unjust, and intolerable'; he accused the government of bringing the law into 'contempt and disrepute'. Non-violent campaigns by the ANC had been met by the state's violence, 'a reign of terror'. In apartheid South Africa Africans faced a conflict between their conscience and the law. He had followed his own conscience and, 'If I had my time over I would do the same again, so would any man who dares call himself a man'. Denied the right to live a normal life he had 'live[d] the life of an outlaw'. He had done his duty to his people and his country. 'I have no doubt,' he concluded, 'that posterity will pronounce that I was innocent and that the criminals that should have been brought before this court are the members of the Verwoerd government.'[44]

African spectators packed the court's public gallery and word of mouth ensured some awareness in black Johannesburg of his speech. White South Africans knew virtually nothing of it: Mandela was banned, his statements could not be quoted and nervous editors ran only the briefest accounts of the trial. In contrast, British and American newspapers reported the speech, marking the start of his international reputation. Mandela was sentenced to five years' imprisonment. His brief career as an outlaw and guerrilla – audacious, flamboyant and reckless – was over. He served most of his sentence in Pretoria, before he was moved to Robben Island for two weeks in mid-1963.

By the close of 1962, underground ANC and MK structures were increasingly ad hoc, incoherent and vulnerable. Mandela was in prison, Sisulu under house arrest and Tambo in London. Police held people for ninety days, in solitary confinement, applying torture techniques learned from France and America. Seasoned activists 'cracked like egg shell';[45] they implicated others. Lines of command and decision-making structures crumpled.

These pressures bore directly on the Liliesleaf hide-out where MK leaders were living, joined by others for tense and sometimes fractious meetings. Just when security should have been at its tightest, it grew lax. It was almost impossible to control comings and goings. Mandela, from prison, sent anxious messages through his lawyers to ensure that the cache of incriminating documents that he had left at Liliesleaf be destroyed. They were not. Clumsily hidden, they were found by police after the Rivonia arrests and became key exhibits in the ensuing trial.

There were tensions, too, among those meeting at the farm. Mbeki and Slovo were the main authors of Operation Mayibuye, an ambitious blueprint for guerrilla war in the countryside leading to 'mass revolutionary action'. The wisdom of the strategy fiercely divided those privy to it. On 11 July a meeting was held to discuss it again. Aware of deteriorating security, those present agreed that this must be the last meeting held on the farm – and so it proved to be. A police raid succeeded beyond the officers' dreams: they arrested the very top layer of those they sought – Sisulu, Mbeki, Kathrada – and discovered a treasure trove of documents, including Operation Mayibuye.

The Rivonia Trial began in October 1963. Mandela, in prison garb, joined the other accused. His appearance shocked observers: the lawyer Joel Joffe thought that 'he had withered during his year in a South African jail, and looked thin and miserably underweight'. The trial has been exhaustively described elsewhere.[46] The defence team was aware from the outset that there was a real prospect of the death sentence for their clients, and they saw two issues as crucial in averting this outcome. They must establish that all MK's sabotage actions had been planned to avoid loss of life, and that Operation Mayibuye (which the prosecution called 'the corner-stone of the state case') had been discussed, but not approved.

The other accused gave lengthy evidence and were extensively cross-examined. Mandela did not enter the witness box, but made his famous statement from the dock. It was an eloquent moral and political riposte to the charges brought against the accused; its famous closing sentences are all the more memorable read against the real possibility of death sentences. In the event, six weeks later, on 12 June 1964, Rusty Bernstein was acquitted and the other eight accused sentenced to life imprisonment. Late that night, Denis Goldberg was taken to the white section of Pretoria Central Prison; Mandela and the others were flown from a military airbase to a cold, wet, windy Robben Island.

4

Prison Years: The Forging of the Steel

Cowards die many times before their deaths;
The valiant never taste of death but once.
Of all the wonders that I yet have heard,
It seems to me most strange that men should fear;
Seeing that death, a necessary end,
Will come when it will come.*

William Shakespeare[47]

*Political prisoners on Robben Island marked their favourite passage in a hidden volume of Shakespeare's plays. This was Mandela's choice.

Robben Island lies 6 miles from Cape Town, a bleak, flat slab of rock and sand as horizontal as Table Mountain across the bay is vertical. For centuries it held those deemed dangerous to mainland society: Muslim leaders from the Dutch East Indies, runaway slaves, Xhosa and Zulu royals; and, into the twentieth century, paupers, 'lunatics' and lepers. In 1961 'the Apartheid regime returned the desolate place of colonial exile and incarceration to its former purgatorial role'.[48] A maximum-security prison was built there: for three decades, it held thousands of political prisoners.[49] For eighteen years it was the physical, political and psychological setting of Mandela's incarceration, before eight years in two mainland prisons.

When the Rivonia men arrived in mid-1964, a policy had been adopted that only white warders would be employed on the island. Most were poorly educated young Afrikaners, crammed with the prejudices of their time and class. The prison held common law and political prisoners, in separate blocks. In 1964, almost all the politicals were PAC members; in the next couple of years, hundreds of ANC members were tried, found guilty, and despatched to Robben Island. By 1965 there were some 800 political prisoners, a majority of them ANC members; this population had halved by 1976, when it rose sharply again.

Mandela and the others were taken to a separate building, known as B Section or the single-cell section. B Section usually held only about thirty inmates, and the prison authorities went to great lengths to prevent any contact between them and the mass of the political prisoners housed in the general sections, in dormitory-type cells. The Rivonia men joined senior PAC members, a handful of ANC activists and half a dozen men from smaller organisations. There were African, Indian and coloured prisoners, each confined in a cell some 8 feet by 7 feet, with only a mat to sleep on and no furniture.

The regime encountered by the new arrivals was vengeful and punitive. Loss of liberty was made more arduous by meagre food, exhausting manual labour – breaking stones in the yard or hacking lime and rock from the quarry – and by a slew of regulations, any contravention of which, actual or imagined, could bring retribution by warders. Punishments ranged from loss of a day's meals to six months in solitary confinement. With one notorious exception, B Section prisoners were not subject to organised assaults or the arbitrary violence prevalent in the general sections; but every day brought its ration of indignity, discomfort and degradation.

Conditions and treatment changed over time. They were harshest in what Neville Alexander called the 'years of hell', 1962 to 1966. (Alexander was a member of an ephemeral revolutionary movement and served ten years

on Robben Island. Alexander – hostile to nationalism –
and Mandela debated political theory intensely whenever
they could.[50]) A mass hunger strike in 1966 won some
improvements: a dining hall was built and organised sport
was permitted at weekends. From 1967 to 1970 there was
a period of 'relatively civilized treatment and a much
more relaxed atmosphere'; there was a relapse in 1971–72,
and then from 1973 onwards physical pressures were
eliminated and treatment became more humane.[51] After
a decade in jail the Rivonia group washed in hot water for
the first time; the diet was more varied, and in 1977 hard
labour was ended. Over time, blatant abuses and violence
were phased out; the behaviour of the warders improved;
prisoners could study, write and receive more letters, and
spend more time in one another's company.

Mandela's own treatment was marginally better
than that of his comrades. When they were flown to the
island, the others were shackled and handcuffed; he was
not. Permission to enrol for a law degree which had been
granted during his two-week stay in 1963 was renewed
when he returned in 1964. Accordingly, his cell alone
had a shelf for reading materials. His diet was modified
on medical grounds. His first protest upon return to
the island was about the standard prison issue of short
trousers, and within days a pair of long trousers appeared
in his cell. 'No pin-striped three-piece suit has ever pleased
me as much,' he wrote, but his demand that the same
concession be extended to his comrades was refused, and
he handed his pair back.[52] (Long trousers were issued to

African prisoners in 1967.) Mandela knew that the favours he enjoyed were potentially divisive, and so he was at pains to press for collective, not individual, amelioration.

The fight for better conditions was a constant of life on the island. Tactics included deputations, memoranda and litigation; go-slow strikes in the quarries; and, as a last resort, hunger strikes. The persistent struggle for improvements and the cumulative effect of each tiny victory were crucially important for the Robben Islanders, perhaps especially for those serving life sentences without the comfort of any release date. They gave a sense of purpose in the pursuit of attainable ends: 'We tried to negotiate collectively. We felt we had something to do,' wrote Mac Maharaj of these years.[53] When any demand succeeded, morale was buoyed; when it was thwarted, resolve was renewed.

Their collective achievement in winning recognition, respect and rights also contributed directly to a sense of community. Many ex-inmates have attested the camaraderie which developed, and an egalitarian ethos. Said Sonny Venkatrathnam, member of a rival organisation, 'Whether it was Nelson or any of the young chaps ... there was always absolute equality in terms of where prison life was concerned.'[54] After twenty-five years in jail, Ahmed Kathrada wrote about striving to change the environment 'brick by brick' to make life more tolerable. This helped create a shared life 'of great warmth, fellowship, friendship, humour and laughter; of strong convictions, of a generosity of spirit, of compassion, solidarity and care … Unbelievably, it is a very positive, confident, determined – yes, even a happy community.'[55]

This sense of community is justly celebrated in the literature on Robben Island. Celebrated, and romanticised, for not all the political prisoners – or even all the ANC prisoners – pulled in the same direction all the time. In part, this was a natural outcome of being in jail alongside one another for years on end. Kathrada noted drily, in a letter written just five years into his sentence: 'Living with the same faces day in and day out must be having adverse psychological effects … We do get on one another's nerves.'[56] In the suffocating confines of prison, minor matters could take root and fester; quarrels damaged relationships. But the natural friction between men thrown so ineluctably together was more easily contained than the acute conflicts that precipitated two political crises. One was within the ANC leadership in B Section; the second pitted their generation against an impatient younger cohort.

Between 1969 and 1975, clashes over policy drove a rift between the ANC leaders in B Section. This was described in a report from Robben Island delivered to the exiled ANC in Lusaka in 1976.[57] Shortly after their arrival, the ANC seniors in B Section created a set of covert structures and committees; at their apex was the High Organ, responsible for policy, behaviour and discipline. Its original members were Mandela, Mbeki, Mhlaba and Sisulu. When these four fell out, other prisoners took sides in the dispute. Within the High Organ, 'the two who represented polar opposites in attitudes and opinions were Madiba and Govan [Mbeki]'.

The High Organ first split over the question of whether the ANC should play any part in the politics of apartheid structures (such as political parties in the Bantustans). Mandela and Sisulu thought there might be strategic grounds for doing so; Mbeki and Mhlaba were opposed on principle. A second, long-running disagreement concerned the relationship of the ANC and the Communist Party. In addition, 'another thorny question which though not openly debated was an undercurrent … was the question of Madiba's status' – expressed as an insistence on collective rather than individual leadership.

How did this arise? Some lodge responsibility at Mbeki's door: he 'was the source of bad blood among the principals', wrote historian Padraig O'Malley; he was 'a hard uncompromising communist, intolerant of opposing opinions', judged Martin Meredith, one of Mandela's biographers. However, Mandela's capacity for discord should not be overlooked. Michael Dingake noted that Madiba was said by some to be 'controversial and dogmatic' and that his 'direct, fiercely candid approach' could leave his opponents bloodied and humiliated. Sisulu agreed: 'He could be harsh with colleagues.' Andrew Masondo recalled that Mandela's interrogatory debating style had upset Joe Gqabi so that 'the relationship between the two of them hardened'.[58]

The stand-off involved issues of principle and policy, but personality, temperament and the unforgiving context also played their part. Each clash fed off the previous one; opposition acquired its own momentum. Unsuccessful attempts to resolve the crisis were initiated by Mbeki in 1970 and 1973. Peace was finally restored in 1975.[59]

The second political crisis on the island was a generational and ideological challenge. After the Soweto uprising of June 1976, there was an influx of younger, angrier and zealously militant prisoners. Many identified themselves with the Black Consciousness movement; others were unaffiliated, but no less combative. These radicals showed scant respect for the Rivonia generation. Mosiuoa Lekota recalled that 'lots of the comrades thought the Rivonia people were old conservatives, and that the PAC was more appealing'. Zithulele Cindi agreed: 'You meet them and they don't match expectations.' The newcomers felt that the older prisoners were too reconciled to their plight and compromised by their relatively good relations with the warders.[60]

Their arrival triggered attempts by both the ANC and the PAC to recruit new members from the new arrivals and precipitated new levels of political rivalry and hostility on the island. The ANC was more successful. One of those who was won over, Mike Xego, explained why: 'One by one, the ANC underground on Robben Island worked on us – on individuals – talking with us and smuggling notes to us.' Mandela was initially shocked by the width of the generation gap – 'to be perceived as a moderate was a novel and not altogether pleasant feeling' – but was determined to bridge it. He did not challenge the 'young lions' for their immaturity and political shallowness, but insisted on meeting them, listening to them and drawing deep on his reservoir of personal persuasiveness.[61]

After these two convulsive challenges to the collective resolve of the Rivonia leaders, by 1978 a relative calm returned. Prisoners agreed a code of conduct prioritising tolerance and disciplined behaviour. Conditions continued to improve. The blanket ban on news was dropped: prisoners could hear radio programmes on an intercom system; by 1980, they received newspapers and magazines. Political discussions no longer required the same levels of secrecy; the island experience, wrote Sampson, 'was like a protracted course in a remote left-wing university'.[62] Mandela used the more flexible social space in various ways. He was devoted to the garden that he and others had been allowed to develop; he resumed work on his law degree in 1980; and he read voraciously.

How did Mandela experience prison? To what uses did he put that experience – and how did the experience shape him? Every prisoner suffered psychological pain in his own way, and often intensely privately. Kathrada wrote, 'Our deepest personal pain was not something we shared with one another.' Mac Maharaj described his desolation, over two years, when he was 'completely listless, very self-pitying, seized with … a state of mental ennui' – a state that he too 'wouldn't want to reveal to my fellow comrades'.[63]

Nelson Mandela shared their reticence about his 'deepest personal pain', but occasionally let it show. Writing on Robben Island, he said:

The worst part of imprisonment is being locked up by yourself. You come face to face with time and there is nothing more terrifying ... Then the ghosts come crowding in. They can be very sinister, very mischievous, raising a thousand doubts in your mind ... Was the sacrifice worth the trouble?[64]

In a 1969 letter, he grieved at the death of his eldest son and his inability to attend the funeral. People might imagine, he continued, that the long sentence, isolation, hard labour, coarse food, boredom and frustrations were the worst features of life in prison, 'But some of us have had experiences much more painful than these, because these experiences eat too deeply into one's being, into one's soul'.[65]

A year later, he wrote to Winnie: 'I feel as if I have been soaked in gall, every part of me, my flesh, bloodstream, bone and soul, so bitter am I to be completely powerless to help you.' And it was to this diagnosis that he returned, in conversation with Richard Stengel, twenty-five years later. Stengel asked what his worst moment on Robben Island had been, and Mandela replied that it was when Winnie was harassed and persecuted 'and I was not there to defend her. That was a very difficult moment for me ... and the feeling of frustration and helplessness was there, because there was nothing I could do about it.'[66]

Mandela was impotent in the face of the state's treatment of his wife: she was banned, detained, held in solitary confinement, brought to the brink of physical and mental collapse; she was spied upon, arrested and jailed. In 1977, she was banished from Soweto to 'little Siberia', as she dubbed the bleak township of the Orange Free State town Brandfort. When she visited him, visibly drained, Mandela was devastated, 'tortured by a sense of guilt and shame', he wrote. But he was equally powerless to intervene as Winnie's behaviour became ever more erratic: reports of drinking and spending, her string of undesirable lovers, her endorsement of 'necklacing' – and much else – reached the island. Although Mandela remained immovably loyal to Winnie, he must, privately, have been visited by a fresh set of sinister and mischievous ghosts.

Winnie remained his emotional lifeline. His letters to her were unfailingly affectionate, frequently confessional, and passionate, quite unlike the formal, slightly flowery style of most of his letters from prison. They make moving reading, their poignancy the more acute with hindsight and the knowledge of the collapse of the dreams after his release. Throughout his prison years, Mandela's family was a source of perplexity and pain. The grief he felt when Thembi died, at just 24 years old, must have been cruelly compounded by the knowledge that the young man had been living in Cape Town but had never made the ferry trip to visit his father. His younger son, Makgatho, dropped out of school and resisted all Mandela's repeated exhortations to complete his education. Mandela knew perfectly well that he had prioritised politics over family, and that those closest to him paid a heavy price for that choice.

What toll was exacted on Mandela by these psychological pressures? There is broad consensus that the years in prison steeled, even hardened, him; that he controlled his emotions tightly, so that self-discipline became a defining characteristic. Maharaj spoke of his 'immense capacity for self-control ... consciously cultivated and nurtured'. Mandela 'changed over the years. I think that in prison his anger and hatred of the system increased, but the manifestations of that anger became less visible. They were subdued, tempered.' Richard Stengel (when working closely with Mandela in the preparation of his autobiography) repeatedly pressed Mandela for his own analysis: 'I used to ask him how prison had changed him. How was the man who came out in 1990 different from the man who entered it in 1962?' Mandela was annoyed by the question, ignoring it or denying its validity. 'Finally, one day, he said to me in exasperation, "I came out mature."' Stengel glosses this convincingly as Mandela harnessing his youthful, impetuous, sensitive side, and filtering all his personal dealings through a learnt restraint, an 'omnipresent filter'.[67]

In a subtle account of Mandela's self-control, literary scholar David Schalkwyk explores its similarities to classical Stoicism. Even those who most admired Mandela noted a sense of distance, making it hard to know him well. His tight management of emotions had advantages, 'but it also brought with it an immense loss of humanity'. Martin Meredith said that Mandela emerged from prison 'an intensely private person, accustomed to concealing his emotions behind a mask'. Indeed, as he wrote to Winnie in 1976, 'I have been fairly successful in putting on a mask behind which I have pined for the family … I am struggling to suppress my emotion as I write this letter.'[68]

After his release from jail in 1990, Mandela confided in few people. He discouraged familiarity. He was often lonely, more cut off than ever from old friendships. 'It was excruciating to see him sitting alone at his big table at home,' a close colleague told Sampson. He recalled that Mandela once told him, 'I have no friends,' and added, 'If you raise a question with emotional overtones he can look stony; you know that you won't get anywhere. He has developed a total politicisation of being. It was a price I wouldn't like to pay.'[69] After 1990 Mandela was most at ease socially with strangers and acquaintances; he discouraged warmth and emotion in his friendships; and his family life was essentially a disaster area. This inversion of the conventional pyramid of affinities speaks of how prison marked the man.

Mandela's strict management of his emotions was the counterpart to the ferocious physical regimen to which he subjected his body. Running on the spot, shadow-boxing, sit-ups and press-ups were all that was possible in his cell; later, he could exercise more expansively outdoors. When he was transferred from Robben Island to Pollsmoor Prison near Cape Town, his mini-gym boasted weights, an exercise bike and natty sportswear donated by the International Red Cross. Regular exercise helped transform the gaunt, sallow figure who had shocked his lawyers before the Rivonia Trial into the trim, upright form who was constantly reported as looking well and younger than his years by his jail visitors. An entry in his prison calendar, a fortnight before his release, noted that his trouser size was still a 34-inch waist: the effects of the emotional discipline were not as easily measured, but equally real.

If austere self-control was a key feature of Mandela's development in prison, another, often remarked upon, was a concern for others, an empathy and ability to listen. He met prisoners individually, giving legal advice, political guidance or counsel on personal issues. He was, said Maharaj, 'very shrewd', taking an interest in every prisoner: 'he would quietly question you – your background, your family, everything.' And not only prisoners: Christo Brand had only recently taken up his job as warder when he first escorted Mandela from B Section to the visitors' centre. Mandela walked ahead of him, and spoke quietly. He did not (as Brand had expected) ask for news or discuss politics. 'All he wanted to know was where I came from, whether my parents were still alive, and to ask if I had any brothers or sisters.' In later encounters, 'when I was alone with him, he drew me in'.[70]

Christo Brand was 20 years old when Mandela disarmed him. It was one moment in a longer, self-conscious and effective strategy. Mandela, from the outset, believed that advantages could be gained by differentiating between the warders. At his urging, the High Organ adopted as policy that warders who treated prisoners fairly and decently should in turn be treated respectfully. If some degree of mutual respect existed, it might narrow the gap between white jailer and black inmate. Dingake noted perceptively that Mandela, 'whether by design or by instinct', behaved differently towards senior and junior officers. With younger men 'who knew their position, Nelson was charming and fatherly'. Some of them reciprocated; they treated him civilly, and at times solicited advice about their jobs and families. By contrast, 'The top officers constituted Madiba's target'.[71]

What began as an attempt to influence the micro politics of the island took on extra dimensions. Mandela might have begun to study the Afrikaans language to facilitate his interactions with the young wardens, but over time he elevated it to a more significant project. In 1975 Mandela wrote that it is a mistake to think all Afrikaners are the same: 'We ought to speak directly to the Afrikaner and fully explain our position. Honest men are to be found on both sides of the colour line and the Afrikaner is no exception.'[72] He began to read Afrikaner history, poetry and novels. Later, during key encounters with senior Afrikaner politicians, Mandela surprised them by his familiarity with their history and culture. It was a card he learned to play, deftly and repeatedly.

For a quarter of a century Mandela's only audience, other than his co-inmates, were Afrikaner prison officers and wardens (and from the mid-1980s politicians and civil servants). Mandela's willingness to engage with these men – offering his respect in return for theirs, winning their trust, assessing their strengths and weaknesses – was, in effect, a dress rehearsal for the role he would play after release. The relationships he established with warders and prison officials were reworked and re-enacted after his release. Mandela's ability to win the trust of Afrikaner hardliners such as General Constand Viljoen was invaluable in the run-up to the 1994 election.

In April 1982 the familiar routines and rhythms on the island were unexpectedly disrupted. With no prior notice, without time to take leave of their comrades, not knowing why they were being moved nor where, Mandela and three other Rivonia men (Sisulu, Mhlaba and Mlangeni – Kathrada joined them a couple of months later) were taken to Pollsmoor Prison in Tokai, on the southern fringe of Cape Town.

Mandela and the four others suddenly enjoyed more spacious quarters, better food and fewer petty restrictions, but they missed the larger community of political prisoners to which they had grown so accustomed on the island. News was no longer censored; so from prison Mandela and the others closely followed political developments. P.W. Botha's 'Total Strategy' was an awkward combination of heightened repression and a modicum of reform – always a risky formula for an authoritarian regime. Mandela and the others were heartened by the formation of the United Democratic Front (UDF) and its ability to mobilise large numbers in protests on an unprecedented scale. The UDF was an umbrella body of organisations opposed to apartheid and broadly supportive of the ANC.

The exiled ANC responded to the militancy, and the accompanying mass arrests, by calling for activists to make South Africa 'ungovernable'.

In January 1985 Botha offered Mandela release if he 'unconditionally rejected violence as a political instrument'. Mandela refused the offer in a speech read at a UDF rally by his daughter, Zindzi: 'Let him [Botha] renounce violence. Let him say he will dismantle apartheid … Only free men can negotiate. Prisoners cannot enter into contracts.' Within these ringing words lurked a rich historical irony. By the end of that year, Mandela was seeking to meet directly with representatives of Botha's government in order to negotiate – from prison.

5

Release and Reconciliation: The Building of a Nation?

History says, Don't hope
On this side of the grave,
But then, once in a lifetime
The longed-for tidal wave
Of justice can rise up,
And hope and history rhyme.

So hope for a great sea-change
In the far side of revenge.
Believe that a further shore
Is reachable from here.
Believe in miracles
And cures and healing wells.*

Seamus Heaney, 1991[73]

*Heaney heard of Mandela's release while working in Harvard on his play, *The Cure at Troy*, and in response 'wrote an extra set of lines for the Chorus'.

The story of Mandela's secret negotiations with representatives of the South African government has been exhaustively recounted.[74] Familiar details include Mandela's meetings with Kobie Coetsee, Minister of Justice, and the commencement early in 1988 of forty-seven meetings between the prisoner and a secret committee of four men. The senior pair on the government side were Coetsee and Niël Barnard, head of the National Intelligence Service (NIS). These were talks about talks: Mandela pressed from the outset for subsequent, formal negotiations between government and ANC. He embarked on this journey very much on his own. Initially, he told no one about his efforts to meet Coetsee: not Sisulu, alongside him in Pollsmoor; not Tambo, head of the exiled movement.

In November 1985, Mandela was relocated in Pollsmoor, to spacious quarters, away from the other Rivonia men. In a much-quoted passage from *Long Walk to Freedom*, Mandela explained that he viewed his new circumstances as 'not a liability but an opportunity': he had concluded that a military victory was 'a distant if not impossible dream … It was time to talk.' It was risky, he knew, but later said, 'There are times when a leader must move out ahead of the flock … confident that he is leading his people the right way.'[75] Perhaps because of this retrospective assertion of individual leadership, there has been a tendency to see these meetings as entirely due to Mandela. This overlooks two crucial things. First, it takes two to tango; second, both partners had good reasons for taking to the floor.

Key individuals within the South African state began meeting Mandela because by the middle of the decade they accepted that, ultimately, negotiations were necessary – that apartheid no longer served white interests. One such actor was the securocrat Barnard, who nudged President Botha towards 'talks about talks'. In 1986, Botha approved Coetsee's informal talks with Mandela – but secretly, without informing the rest of the Cabinet, and in 1988, Barnard's committee began its sequence of meetings with Mandela on Botha's authority.

The NIS was a sophisticated intelligence machine, moving in directions quite different from those of the military command and Botha. Barnard and his deputy, Mike Louw, believed that white interests were better served by a political settlement than by protracted military action: 'the sooner we negotiated a new system the better.' From about 1983, in-house NIS papers advocated Mandela's release and the unbanning of the ANC as precursors to negotiations. Mandela's release would not only facilitate the possibility of talks, but would also serve to demystify him – the NIS was keen to avoid the Ayatollah Khomeini effect.[76]

What impelled the NIS, the Cabinet reformers, and ultimately Botha himself to negotiate with the ANC? Essentially, by the 1980s, the National Party was in crisis: the apartheid project had run its course. The South African economy had never recovered from the international recession of the 1970s; politically, apartheid was badly wounded in the 1970s by an assertive Black Consciousness movement, the Soweto revolt and the mobilisation of black workers in trade unions. From 1984, the rolling protests mounted by the UDF marked new levels of militancy. The NP was haemorrhaging white voter support to the left and right; internationally, the regime was subject to a credit squeeze, sanctions and disinvestment.

For its part, the ANC called off armed struggle in favour of talks with 'the enemy' primarily because of the international context. Historically, the Soviet bloc had supported MK generously, providing training, arms and money, but by 1986 Moscow sought political solutions to African conflicts and signalled that it was reducing military aid. In 1988, Angola closed all the MK camps within its boundaries. Armed struggle relying on external support and forward bases was no longer feasible. By 1989, the exiled ANC leadership privately acknowledged that it no longer had the capacity 'to intensify the armed struggle in any meaningful way'. Both the NP and ANC entered negotiations for want of a feasible alternative.

Key individuals within the ANC, including Mandela, arrived at this conclusion earlier than others. Among the exiled leadership, Thabo Mbeki decided early on that a negotiated deal was a more likely outcome than a seizure of power. He was in Lusaka in 1985 when ANC members sat down with leading South African business leaders, and from November 1987 he and carefully selected ANC colleagues met a small group of Afrikaner intellectuals in a series of meetings to explore the possibility of formal negotiations. Mbeki's attendance was approved by Oliver Tambo, but not broadly known in the ANC; the academic Willie Esterhuyse and his colleagues reported to Niël Barnard.[77]

In short, from 1985 onwards, 'a faint whiff of negotiations was constantly in the air'.[78] Mandela's clandestine encounters with Coetsee and Barnard ran in parallel with those taking place in London and Lusaka. Not so much a tango, then, as a complicated quadrille – but all those involved were dancing to the same music.

Mandela finally met Botha in July 1989. They spent a cordial couple of hours together but there was not time for the relationship to develop. A month later, Botha's Cabinet colleagues forced his resignation. The new president was F.W. de Klerk. It was he who opened parliament on 2 February 1990 with the dramatic news that the ANC, PAC and SACP were unbanned with immediate effect, that Mandela's release was imminent and that his government would seek to negotiate a democratic constitution. In 1993, de Klerk and Mandela were jointly awarded the Nobel Peace Prize.

Born into an Afrikaner political family, de Klerk first entered parliament in 1972 and Cabinet six years later, shifting gradually from the right wing of the NP to its *verligte* (reformist) wing. Balding, genial and direct in manner, de Klerk fitted the term 'avuncular' as if it had been coined to describe him. During the years of negotiations, he emerged as a tactician rather than a strategist, and many Afrikaners believed that he conceded too much, too readily. De Klerk's place in history is assured by his association with Mandela in the 1990s; his historical reputation is diminished by comparison with the iconic figure.

Mandela and de Klerk never enjoyed a close relationship – or each other's company. At their very first meeting, an aide noted, 'there was no warmth between the two men'.[79] Both spoke, and subsequently wrote, about the other in ungenerous and critical terms. Mandela's famous charm and ability to win over Afrikaners conspicuously failed in this instance. The most fraught moments in the entire negotiation process took place when their mutual distrust flared into public rancour.

Mandela was released from prison on 11 February 1990. Despite elaborate planning, the event flirted with fiasco. A vast crowd thronged the sweltering Grand Parade in Cape Town, waiting for hours. An unruly fringe began to loot shop windows; police fired rubber bullets and shotgun rounds. When Mandela's car finally arrived, hours later than scheduled, excitement overrode order. People leaped on the car, hammered at is windows, shaking it – so that the driver retreated to the suburbs, before a second, slightly more orderly arrival. Summer light was fading when Mandela, from the balcony of the old town hall, spoke in public for the first time since the Rivonia Trial.

The speech was formulaic and its delivery wooden. Its most memorable line was an attempt to moderate messianic expectations: 'I stand here before you not as a prophet but as a humble servant of you, the people.' Mandela declared himself 'a loyal and disciplined member' of the ANC; he pledged to sustain the armed struggle and reiterated the Freedom Charter's promise to nationalise the mines. A global television audience marvelled at the sight of Mandela, but few were uplifted or stirred by what he said.

Just twelve hours later a strikingly different Mandela was on display at an early morning press conference. Facing 200 experienced and hard-nosed journalists from across the world, he delivered 'an exercise in seduction … a master class in political persuasion'. Every question elicited a superbly pitched response. Mandela's characteristic delivery later became familiar – the self-deprecating humour, the formal diction, the blend of gravitas and glamour – but it thrilled on first airing. When the conference ended, wrote John Carlin, 'something happened I had never seen before … in thirty years reporting on politicians. Hypnotising us into forgetting we were working journalists, making a mockery of our pretensions to objectivity, he drew from us a long burst of spontaneous, heartfelt applause.'[80]

With hindsight, these first two appearances by the released Mandela predicted much that took place over the next few years. They foretold that Mandela would become the ANC's greatest asset – able to excite the masses and to confer legitimacy and respectability on the movement. They provided the first glimpses of a consummate political operator, keenly aware of the aura attached to him, and intent on using it to lever every inch of advantage for his cause. They explain his political priorities: first, to rally forces loyal to the ANC and enlist them for negotiations and the cessation of violence; second, to embark on a tireless round of foreign travel, raising funds and winning support for a liberation movement that had become effectively a government-in-waiting.

In the weeks after his release Mandela addressed huge crowds at rallies in all the major cities. His message was carefully crafted: on the one hand, militant – 'Now is the time to intensify the struggle on all fronts' – and on the other hand, calming, calling for discipline. What he said was largely ignored by adoring, chanting crowds. These were not so much political mass meetings as euphoric celebrations. Soweto, Port Elizabeth and Bloemfontein were successive staging posts for 'Mandela's coronation as king of black South Africa'.[81]

His reception was very different in Durban. His visit took place against the backdrop of vicious fighting in KwaZulu Natal between Zulu-speakers loyal to Inkatha (headed by Chief Mangosuthu Buthelezi) and those enlisted in the colours of the UDF, for long a surrogate for the ANC. Inkatha was originally a cultural movement, imbued with a patriarchal, conservative Zulu traditionalism; some of its members were armed and trained by the NP's security forces to combat the UDF; in 1990, Buthelezi relaunched it as the Inkatha Freedom Party, aiming at a national following. Mandela, writes Ari Sitas, was 'adamant and provocative': he told a predominantly youthful crowd of ANC supporters to 'take your guns, your knives, and your pangas, and throw them into the sea ... End this war now!' Many in his audience were 'angry and devastated [at] ... being given a lecture by an out of touch patriarch'.[82]

Given Mandela's subsequent standing as virtually beyond reproach, it is worth recalling that in the first couple of years after his release his authority in the ANC was contested, not taken for granted. Some UDF leaders still fretted at Mandela's secret meetings with government. In KwaZulu Natal, local ANC leaders blocked Mandela from meeting Buthelezi and negotiating directly with him. Activists were concerned that their icon was more conservative and more out of touch than they had expected. Within ANC structures Mandela was criticised for his autocratic style and failure to consult, and for being too close to de Klerk. However, at the ANC's National Conference in July 1991, Mandela's election as president of the ANC was uncontested and wildly applauded.

Outside South Africa, Mandela's reception was overwhelmingly positive. Between his release and mid-1992, he visited forty-nine countries on sixteen separate trips. Nowhere was his progress more triumphal than in the USA in June 1990. Eight cities, from coast to coast, in eleven days; the largest ticker-tape reception New York had ever seen; the first African and third private citizen to address Congress. Everywhere he was received by his African-American hosts with messianic fervour. He was a modern Moses, said New York's first black mayor, David Dinkins. 'We have a new Jerusalem,' cried church leader Benjamin Chavis. Mandela laid a wreath at Martin Luther King's tomb; he began every speech with a roll-call of black American heroes and martyrs – and he raised over $7 million for the ANC.[83]

Back in South Africa, Mandela was only sporadically involved in direct talks. These were handled by Cyril Ramaphosa, Thabo Mbeki, Joe Slovo, Valli Moosa and others. The first meeting between the ANC and NP members was in May 1990; in August, the ANC made the vital concession of ending its armed struggle, and in December 1991 formal negotiations commenced. Progress was interrupted and at moments derailed by persistent violence, as Inkatha and ANC loyalists fought a low-level civil war in Johannesburg's townships and in KwaZulu Natal but, if anything, the disruptions emphasised the need for agreement.

The negotiated settlement produced an interim constitution and bill of rights. It agreed a date for a general election based on universal franchise and provided for a subsequent Government of National Unity (GNU) in which any party winning twenty seats or more would serve. The settlement guaranteed security of tenure for white civil servants and approved that amnesty be offered to members of the security forces in exchange for full disclosure of abuses of power – the basis of the Truth and Reconciliation Commission.

Alongside the negotiations on constitutional arrangements, a less formal series of discussions on the economy were conducted between economic and political elites. They agreed on the need for macro-economic stability and the opening of the economy to international trade and finance: the prevailing globalisation orthodoxy. By accepting the 'Washington Consensus', the ANC jettisoned social democratic measures such as pro-poor spending and progressive taxation. In return for leaving the citadels of capital unthreatened, the ANC won an undertaking from big business to accelerate the entry of black shareholders into their boardrooms.

Arguably, the ANC's acquiescence in the interests of big business in the transition period has been the decisive constraint on its performance in government since 1994. If so, to what extent was Nelson Mandela responsible for the ANC's embrace of prevailing economic orthodoxy? He did not author the ANC's shuffle from centre-left to centre-right on the economy, but his role was crucial in effecting it, in two main respects. First, he appears to have been especially open to the blandishments and persuasion of business interests at a personal level. He enjoyed the glamour of wealth in much the same way that he revelled in the glitz of show business and was 'showered with a small financial fortune by friendly tycoons'.[84]

Second, Mandela's moral authority and political clout were crucial in winning acceptance for a negotiated outcome that fell short of the expectations of the ANC's supporters. He personified the ANC's rightwards shuffle over the economy. On release, he insisted that departure from the policy of nationalisation of banks and mines was 'inconceivable', but at Davos in February 1992 he unilaterally removed nationalisation from the ANC's agenda, promising to take the steps 'necessary to ensure business confidence'. His change of heart was sincere enough but it translated into an insistence that the rest of the ANC should share his views. The crucial role played by Mandela, and by his adversary-cum-partner de Klerk, was 'to market a grand historical compromise', embodying and translating the contradictions of the process into a credible vision and morally legible narrative.[85]

Mandela also made a series of calls for forgiveness and conciliation as first steps to nation-building. He insisted that he bore no bitterness, that he forgave his jailers and that he sought common ground with white South Africans. He reiterated this stance on countless occasions – and he performed it. It was after his election as president that the most famous instances in the politics of gesture took place: the 'reconciliation lunch' for widows of Afrikaner politicians and their black opponents; a visit to have tea with Betsie Verwoerd, too frail to attend the lunch; and of course the appearance in a Springbok rugby shirt – when the team lifted the World Cup, white rugby supporters chanted 'Nelson, Nelson', and South Africans of all races wept with joy and disbelief.

In the run-up to the 1994 election, Mandela was hard at work allaying white fears, urging blacks to follow his example, constantly using his skills – his memory for names, the warmth of his presence, a deliberate inclusiveness – to conjure respect and affection. That this repertoire was deliberately and consciously deployed does not detract from its effectiveness. Mandela was superb at the politics of gesture because he understood it; he used it to win support, and it worked because he was sincere in wanting it to work. As the historian Bill Freund noted in an obituary, his ability to disarm and to charm meant playing 'a role for which he developed the perfect personality'. A future in which South Africans of all shades shared a common vision proved to be a prospect both fragile and short-lived. But while it lasted, pregnant with possibility, buoyed by belief in 'Madiba magic', it created a political and emotional space that made reconciliation imaginable, 'an unprecedented habitus of hopefulness that spanned the old chasms of race'.[86]

Unsurprisingly, the ANC fought the 1994 election by maximising Mandela's appeal. The party mounted a slick, effective campaign, crafting an inclusive 'liberation narrative' with Mandela as its emblem, its hero. The ANC presented itself as an agent for change rather than a 'liberation movement'; its central message modulated from 'Now is the Time' to 'A Better Life for All'. Mandela's image was consciously softened. A poster used in the closing months of the campaign had a smiling Mandela, in a trademark 'Madiba shirt', with eleven wide-eyed children of all races: not so much 'The People's Choice' (as an earlier poster had it) as the people's grandfather.

Mandela's presidential inauguration was saturated in symbolism. New flag, new anthem and new president were honoured. Dramatically, the new commander-in-chief was saluted by a flypast of military jet fighters. But running for office was easier than running the country; being president was more difficult than becoming president. It meant heading a GNU coalition, a compromise structure symbolised by its deputy presidents, Mbeki and de Klerk. Of thirty Cabinet members, only six NP survivors had prior governmental experience. One of them, businessman Derek Keys, remained Finance Minister. His was a telling appointment, as was the retention of fiscally hawkish Chris Stals as governor of the Reserve Bank. Mandela was determined to calm the currency markets and to woo foreign investors.

A crucial element of the script for Mandela's presidency had, in effect, been written. The ANC campaigned in 1994 on the Reconstruction and Development Programme (RDP), an ambitious manifesto promising broad, vague social reforms. Two years later, the RDP was unceremoniously replaced by the Growth, Employment and Redistribution (GEAR) programme. Enthusiastically welcomed by big business, GEAR was an exercise in fiscal self-discipline: government spending was cut, services outsourced and foreign exchange controls swept away. A million jobs were shed in the public sector, mining, agriculture and manufacturing over the next three years.

The GEAR shift was championed by Thabo Mbeki, to whom Mandela increasingly delegated executive responsibility. Mbeki chaired most Cabinet meetings and oversaw the routine administration of government. Thabo Mbeki was a key player in the transition from apartheid. In exile, he seemed ever present at meetings with Afrikaner politicians and opinion-makers, who were 'charmed and bedazzled by this brilliant, thoughtful, lucid man'; he was adept and subtle during meetings, warm and winning with whisky glass and pipe in hand at the end of the day.[87] Back in South Africa from 1990, Mbeki seemed to be indispensable to the ANC's cause – 'Mr Delivery', a cartoonist called him – although once in office as vice president he became pricklier, less tolerant of opposing views and easily angered. In 1997 he succeeded Mandela as president of the ANC, and it was clear that he would follow the older man as national president too.

As president, Mandela continued to travel extensively. He intervened, with uneven success, in aspects of foreign policy; he delighted in personal diplomacy, confident that phone calls to heads of state would be taken. He enjoyed making appointments to ambassadorial posts, with old loyalties sometimes trumping good judgement. He shuffled his Cabinet reluctantly, tolerating poor performers, although he was swift to dismiss those, like Pallo Jordan and Bantu Holomisa, whose loyalty he doubted.

His colleagues in government were amused or shocked, according to temperament, by the attention he lavished on celebrities (especially women): pop stars, actors, models, beauty queens and sportsmen beyond count all had their photo opportunity with Madiba. It was often difficult to determine who was more star-struck. Mandela, remarked Sampson, 'was not always fastidious in his friendships'.[88] He accepted favours and largesse in a regal way: a home built for him here, a daughter's eye-wateringly lavish wedding paid for there. Mandela also behaved like a chief accepting tribute when it came to fundraising, especially for his personal project to build a hundred schools and fifty clinics. His personal assistant, Zelda la Grange, has given a vivid account of his modus operandi. A handpicked CEO would be invited to breakfast or lunch, or flown out to survey the selected rural site – and the sum of money needed was then specified. Hardly anyone declined. Many of the sites for these buildings were proposed by local chiefs, and Mandela found these requests difficult to resist. This blend of fundraising, philanthropy and aristocratic fiat had its drawbacks. It transpired that, by 1999, 'many of these structures were left abandoned' due to lack of infrastructure, personnel, supplies and know-how.[89]

Mandela's willingness to call in favours set a poor example to others in his party. It was during his presidency that the first alarming signs of patronage and corruption commenced. It was on his watch that the arms deal – a multibillion-rand purchase, controversial at the time and infamous in retrospect – was brokered, the well of governance poisoned. In particular, Mandela permitted Joe Modise to remain as Defence Minister long after rumours and allegations about kickbacks and conflict of interests began to swirl.

As head of government Mandela's record was patchy at best. His crowning political achievement was neither legislative nor executive, but a creative project of 'improvising a nation'.[90] Mandela made a 'new' South African nation imaginable. He was able, writes Deborah Posel, 'to stand in for and enact this "new" people as if it had already come into being'. In the roller-coaster ride of the early 1990s – lurching years of transition, uncertainty and anxiety – what Nelson Mandela did and said, what he came to represent, gave South Africans something to hold on to. He crafted a narrative of redemption and renewal, giving South Africans something to believe in. As icon and as political maestro, he played a role at a particular moment for which he was singularly equipped. As his old intellectual sparring partner on Robben Island, Neville Alexander, put it: 'the new South Africa had become inevitable and would have happened even without Mandela. It would, however, have been a very different place and it would have taken very much longer to come about.'[91]

Alongside the public triumphs, Mandela's private life in the 1990s was bleak and distressing. Although Winnie was at his side for his early public appearances, it was soon apparent that such proximity was for political effect rather than personal intimacy. Despite Mandela's obvious affection for her, their return to married life was disastrous. Having retained a closeness through the prison years, wrote Fatima Meer, 'in their togetherness they began to discover how apart they had become'.[92] They kept different hours, had different lifestyles and different priorities. Winnie made little attempt to conceal her liaisons with other men or to curb her expensive tastes.

Mandela also had to come to terms with Winnie as a controversial and divisive political figure in her own right. The beautiful and generous young woman who had captivated him three decades ago was tougher, harsher and more erratic. Her treatment by the regime had 'turned her from a warm-hearted person into a mad creature', the politician Helen Suzman told Anthony Sampson. If Winnie had always been 'part flint and part flower' (as an American journalist described her), by the time of Mandela's release the flintiness dominated. He was still in prison when she was repudiated in 1989 by the UDF because of her role in a reign of violence and the death of a teenage activist. In 1991, she was convicted on kidnapping charges, although she remained popular in some circles, particularly militant youth groups and ex-MK members. In April 1992, Mandela – flanked by his oldest friends, Sisulu and Tambo – held a press conference to announce that he and Winnie were separating.[93]

In 1994 Winnie was appointed Deputy Minister of Arts in Mandela's first Cabinet. Further scandal and improprieties followed, and in March 1995 Mandela dismissed her. Months later he initiated divorce proceedings, hoping to settle the matter privately. Winnie refused. An acrimonious court hearing ensued. It must have been excruciating for one who governed his emotions so stringently to reveal his private life so explicitly. Ever since he had left prison, 'not once has the defendant ever entered the bedroom whilst I was awake … I was the loneliest man during the period I stayed with her.'[94]

Mandela's relations with his children offered scant compensation for the wreckage of his marriage. Zindzi and Zenani found it difficult to communicate with Mandela and remained loyal to their mother, Winnie. His children by his first wife – daughter Maki and son Makgatho – were also wary and had only sporadic contact with their father. Mandela enjoyed slightly better relations with his grandchildren. Makgatho's four sons stayed in his official residence in Pretoria, 'but he was a reserved disciplinarian which often did not go down very well with the young ones'.[95]

Mandela's frequent isolation and loneliness were assuaged when he fell in love again, with Graça Machel, widow of the first president of independent Mozambique. She and Mandela met in 1992; by mid-decade, secret assignations in Paris and elsewhere progressed to a more public liaison. Graça would spend two weeks a month with him in Johannesburg, and by 1997 she was the president's consort, accompanying him on official trips overseas. 'I'm in love with a remarkable lady,' Mandela gravely told a television interviewer in February 1998, and on the morning of his eightieth birthday, that July, they were married by a Methodist bishop in their new home in Houghton. The next evening, at a giant birthday celebration, Mandela began his speech: 'My wife and I' – and 2,000 guests burst into applause.

6

Last Years and Legacy:
Remembering Mandela

He stands on an ancient threshold.
One foot in the commune, one foot
In a once barely emergent aristocracy.
No easy walk.
And so he walks, stolid, uneasily-easily,
Through this cynical end of the 20th century,

Ranging the globe with arcane values:
Of honour, pride, stubbornness, dignity
And a tradition of leadership to be earned
Only in daily communion with a people.

Something like all of this could get lost
After Mandela goes.

Jeremy Cronin[96]

A rainbow is an optical illusion. It is light reflected and refracted through water droplets, seen only when one is positioned in a certain way relative to the sun. It is evanescent, the spectrum of colours fading as the source of the light shifts. The 'rainbow nation' was almost as fleeting, and today is often lamented as an illusion, an unattainable ideal.

The 'rainbow nation of God' (the phrase popularised by Archbishop Tutu in December 1991) invoked a divinely favoured South Africa, diverse yet unified, emerging from a dreadful past but able to transcend that history through forgiveness and atonement. For a few years in the mid-1990s it was a powerful metaphor, made credible by the moral authority and personal appeal of Mandela. But by the late 1990s the metaphor had begun to fray.

White South Africans, grateful though they were to Madiba, by and large failed to realise that reconciliation required more from them than they were prepared to give. Black South Africans, proud though they were of Madiba, felt that he was too accommodating of white fears and not attentive enough to the scar tissue of apartheid's victims.

In December 1997 the ANC held its fiftieth National Conference in Mafikeng. Mandela retired as ANC president (succeeded by Thabo Mbeki) and used the occasion to deliver a four-hour speech which delighted the delegates but disconcerted many commentators at home and overseas. It signalled a distinct change of gear: 'Gone was the gentle, national conciliator,' observed Tony Leon, leader at the time of the opposition Democratic Party (DP); instead, Mandela lambasted 'the anti-democratic forces of counter revolution', including the NP, DP, obstructive civil servants, hostile NGOs and the mass media.[97] The tone accurately heralded a shift in direction under Mbeki's future presidency (unsurprisingly, as the speech was authored by Mbeki and his associate Netshitenzhe). It also signalled that the rainbow had dimmed.

Eighteen months later, in June 1999, the general election saw the ANC win 66 per cent of the vote. Mbeki was installed as president. Mandela told a series of interviewers that he welcomed retirement: 'I want to live in obscurity. I would like to retire to my village.' But he was 'too addicted to life on the public stage' to efface himself in that way, too much in demand ever to attain obscurity.[98] Instead, Mandela spent the next five years – Mbeki's first term – travelling, fundraising, peace-making. He was restlessly active, in a way that few octogenarians could sustain. His first trip in 'retirement' was a swing through half a dozen states in the Middle East, and then as many cities in the USA. A couple of months later he travelled to Burundi on the first of several trips to the Central African country as it recovered from civil war. Mandela engaged energetically in the process of devising transitional arrangements and installing a national unity administration. At one point he flew from Burundi to London (to thank the queen for making him an honorary QC) – for one night! – and then back to Cape Town for a farewell party for Mamphela Ramphele. In November and December 2001 Mandela visited nine countries on three continents.

Much of the travel was geared to raising funds for his three 'legacy foundations': the Children's Fund, the Mandela Foundation and the Mandela Rhodes Foundation. However, as la Grange reveals, Mandela enjoyed travel and 'accepted invitations for no good reason and invented visits because he was determined to fundraise'.[99] Even back in South Africa he was often on the move. He and Graça divided their time between homes in Johannesburg, Qunu and Maputo; Mandela also grew fond of the privacy afforded by Shambala, the house built for him by the insurance magnate Douw Steyn on his game reserve in the Waterberg Mountains north of Johannesburg.

In June 2004 he held a press conference to announce that his appearances would be 'severely and significantly reduced', telling the journalists that he was 'retiring from retirement … don't call me, I'll call you'.

Mandela and Mbeki had a political relationship that fluctuated between distant and abrasive during the younger man's first term.[100] Mbeki resented working in the huge shadow cast by his predecessor; he believed that Mandela's version of national reconciliation was simplistic and moralising, ignoring the need for socio-economic change, and he was stung to the quick by what he termed 'Mandela exceptionalism'. This was the tendency of the media and the white elite to hear, see and speak no evil of the former president, while being ever alert to the shortcomings of other ANC politicians. For his part, Mandela fretted about how little access he had to the office of the president and found it galling to have phone calls unreturned. But their relationship was damaged more fundamentally over Mbeki's stance on HIV AIDS.

Towards the end of his presidency, Mandela apologised to AIDS activists, admitting that he had neglected the issue. As ex-president, he threw himself into the fight against the disease and its associated stigmas. Inevitably, this ranged him against the denialist position Mbeki championed until he was forced by others in the ANC to back down. Mandela launched his 466/64 campaign (named after his number as a prisoner on Robben Island) to help combat the syndrome. His foundation funded programmes administering retroviral therapy, and in December 2001 he criticised Mbeki publicly, charging him with dereliction of duty. Mbeki took his revenge at an ANC National Executive meeting in March 2002 when a choreographed rebuke was delivered by a series of speakers who accused Mandela of 'indiscipline' in raising the matter outside the party's own structures.

In 2004 Mandela was a trump card in the South African Football Association's bid to stage the World Cup. He flew to Grenada to influence the crucial meeting of CONCACAF, the governing body for football in the

Americas and the Caribbean. The day before the final vote in Zurich, Mandela and Mbeki had secret talks in a hotel with Jack Warner, the perennial football fixer – and secured (according to an insider) the three votes he controlled. South Africa edged out the favourite, Morocco, by fourteen votes to ten. It was Mandela's last really vigorous engagement. By 2004 he had become visibly frail, walking with difficulty; by 2006 he was increasingly prone to forgetfulness. As the natural infirmities of age reduced his mobility and capacities, Mandela's public life tapered down.

In 2005 Mandela made his last trip to the USA, where he enjoyed time with Bill Clinton and the Saudi ambassador, Prince Bandar, both of whom were part of an inner circle of associates. He had an awkward meeting with George W. Bush, and briefly met a youthful Senator Obama. In 2007 he was pressed by Prince Albert of Monaco to attend a fundraising event. Although he was tired of travelling, 'when royalty invited him, he was more eager to agree', divulges la Grange.[101] He combined this trip with one to London to attend the unveiling of his statue in Parliament Square. London also hosted his last ever overseas visit: in July 2008, on the occasion of his ninetieth birthday, which was celebrated with a concert in Hyde Park and a highly profitable fundraising dinner.

Not all of Mandela's financial affairs had such successful outcomes. He became anxious about supporting his extended family and maintaining his residences, and he sought advice about generating income. A trust fund was set up which, between 2002 and 2005, received R18.5 million (about £1.7 million at the time) although, as an obituarist commented, 'There does not appear to be a charitable dimension to this fund outside the Mandela family.' Mandela was also persuaded – or inveigled – into fundraising ventures that 'bordered on the tawdry', such as the marketing of golden replicas of his hand and the sale of items of his 'artwork' which were nothing of the kind.[102] Before he fell out with the lawyer Ismail Ayob over the artworks scheme, it emerged that Mandela had signed an agreement transferring copyrights and trademarks using his name to a company owned by Ayob.

After he turned 90, some of Mandela's public appearances occurred only after intense pressure by others. One notorious incident, in October 2008, saw him whisked by plane to the Eastern Cape by his grandson, Mandla, to share a platform with Jacob Zuma, victor over Mbeki in the internecine conflict for the presidency. The flight flouted security provisions and involved a dangerous landing – to the fury of other family members and staff. In 2009, the Mandela Foundation announced that he would take no active part in the general election campaign. But political pressures prevailed and a frail, silent Mandela appeared at an ANC election rally in Soweto, his words pre-recorded. There was further family feuding about whether or not he should attend the opening of the FIFA World Cup in June 2010; his great-granddaughter Zenani died in a car crash on the eve of the event, and this was given as his reason for not attending. However, he was prevailed upon to grace the closing ceremony, in July – driven round the field in a golf buggy, his wife helping lift his arm so that he could wave to the rapturous crowd.[103] It was his final public appearance.

Shortly afterwards, Mandela's physical decline precipitated intense jostling among those close to him. There were clashes between his medical team and the security team; between family, household staff and the Mandela Foundation; and between Graça and other family members. In January 2011 he was hospitalised. By the end of the year he was deemed well enough to return to Qunu. His office at the foundation was closed, personal staff were laid off; his personal assistant of many years believed that 'the poison within the family was leaking out everywhere'.[104]

There is little cheer in recalling the last two years of Mandela's life. It was partly a chronicle of ill-health: he was in and out of hospital, and in the final months his condition was euphemistically described as 'serious but stable', as medical technology and an old man's will power kept him alive. It was partly a shrill soap opera, with family factions clawing for control, ostracising anyone whom they feared might compete with them for a share of the posthumous rewards of being a Mandela. It was a dark comedy: gothic overtones were provided by Mandla Mandela, who disinterred the remains of Mandela's sons and infant daughter and moved them from Qunu to Mveso – until forced by a court to return them. At which point he 'prised open the family closet and revealed the skeletons stacked in it': Mandla's aunts were scheming to control Mandela's income; his brother Ndaba was illegitimate; his ex-wife had borne not his, but his brother Mbuso's son – and so on.[105]

One of the lowest moments in the entire bathetic arc came in April 2013 when President Zuma, Cyril Ramaphosa and other party seniors indulged in a grotesque photo-op as Mandela recuperated after ten days in hospital. Video footage was broadcast on the public television channel: an immobile Mandela, propped in an armchair, while Zuma and the others gurned to camera. If the intention was once more to sprinkle a few drops of Madiba magic on the ANC, it backfired. Public opinion was hostile. Winnie voiced the popular view: 'It was insensitive, it compromised the family, compromised his dignity and it should have never been done.'[106]

These unedifying and undignified episodes were in large part a battle over Mandela's image: about controlling his legacy, owning his name, profiting by association, staking out claims to the icon as he approached death. Squalid they may have been, nevertheless these competing claims introduce a much larger question: how should Mandela be remembered?

This book has circled back to where it began: with the challenge of extricating the person of Mandela from a pervasive – almost limitless – sense of Mandela; distinguishing between the actual, historical individual and a generalised and essentially mythical figure. This task raises questions about memory, reputation and renown. How will Mandela be remembered by historians and by the general public? Which Mandela will persist in popular sentiment – in South Africa, and more broadly?

Such questions are important because Mandela can all too easily be misremembered, recalled in ways that are both simplistic and overblown. They honour a giant, but one which on closer inspection turns out to be a vast cardboard cut-out, a two-dimensional hero lacking depth or complexity. Remembering Mandela in this way tends to exaggerate either his goodness or his greatness – or both – investing the giant with superhuman virtues and powers.

Such hyperbole and rhetorical overkill permeated the obituaries and eulogies when Mandela died. South African commentators hailed him as 'a twin brother of Jesus' and referred to his 'works on earth'. The Irish magnate Tony O'Reilly used the same imagery: Madiba had been 'sent by God'. Secular claims were every bit as ambitious. One commentator judged that transformation in South Africa had been 'orchestrated by one man'; another likened Mandela to Gandhi, Lennon and JFK in a single sentence. Barack Obama is not often outpaced when it comes to the oratorical moment. He declared that Mandela 'has changed the arc of history, transforming his country, the continent and the world'.

Paradoxically, in elevating Mandela to unattainable proportions, the effect is to make him less accessible, less interesting and less credible. He is remembered 'in ways that emaciate, distort and even destroy' his actual legacy.[107]

A complex personality and prodigious career are reduced to a series of abstract nouns: forgiveness, conciliation, peace and love. This kind of recall strips the historical figure of other facets of his personality – stubbornness, loneliness, vanity, a peremptory and even authoritarian edge – and also omits crucial dimensions of his career. It airbrushes out the angry young Africanist, the left-leaning nationalist close to socialist friends and ideas, the militant who gladly headed an underground armed force – and the consummate, calculated politician of later years, persuader nonpareil. Mandela was a much more versatile figure than the cardboard giant.

If one avoids both the exaggerated superhero and the saintly father figure, what kind of historical assessments of Nelson Mandela might fairly be attempted? As he recedes further into the historical past, as more perspectives become available, how might his career be interpreted, his reputation recalibrated? My own suggestions – preliminary and tentative – consider the several major roles that Mandela played: revolutionary and guerrilla; African nationalist leader; negotiator and manager of transition; head of government; and, more abstractly, defender of democracy and champion of a new constitutional order.

Any number of overblown statements portray Mandela as a revolutionary. The SACP declaimed on the day after his death that Comrade Mandela was 'one of the greatest revolutionaries of the twentieth century'.[108] He was not. His active career as a 'revolutionary' – underground operative, trainee guerrilla and MK commander-in-chief – lasted about sixteen months, from March 1961 to his arrest in August 1962. Six months of this were spent out of the country and included several weeks of military training. In all this, Mandela displayed courage and daring, but (like his colleagues at the Rivonia hideaway) he was also reckless, imprudent and careless. More importantly, for the bulk of his political career Mandela was not a revolutionary at all, in any standard meaning of the term. He was committed to ending apartheid, but not to overthrowing the capitalist system in South Africa. According to Neville Alexander, based on discussions on Robben Island, for Mandela the turn to armed struggle was a way of putting pressure on the apartheid regime and not a route to seizure of power. By his own account, Mandela moved decisively away from any idea of military victory and instead towards negotiated political change.

Far more clear-cut is Mandela's standing as one of the most important African nationalist leaders of the twentieth century. He ranks with Nkrumah, Nyerere, Kenyatta, Senghor and Touré in his association with independence from colonial rule – or in South Africa, the end of white minority rule. Indeed, compared with the British and French colonial powers, the National Party in South Africa resisted black majority rule for much longer and through more draconian means. Each of these men was the first president of their new state: Mandela stands out for having served only one term, and for supporting multi-party democracy and the rule of law.

Chapter 5 considered Mandela as negotiator, as personifying the transition, and as head of state from 1994 to 1999. It is for his role in the mid-1990s that his historical reputation is likely to be most lasting. He bestrode the national stage, before and after the 1994 election. More than any other politician he represented the aspirations of the disenfranchised majority and yet was able to reassure white South Africans that they could be part of the new order. His personal appeal and his exemplary ethical behaviour were key components in the makeshift structures of trust built over the deep divides of South African society. The world's media was entranced by the South African drama playing out so publicly, and the narrative came with its own easily identified hero.

To mention Mandela's global acclaim is also to identify an important caveat when it comes to a historical assessment of his role during the 'Madiba Decade'. The international praise that he earned must be offset by serious reservations closer to home, particularly among black South Africans. As the author Zakes Mda wrote, in a *New York Times* obituary short of the reverence displayed in so many others, 'there is an increasingly vocal segment of black South Africans who feel that Mandela sold out the liberation struggle to white interests'. In 1993 a young black truck driver told Jeremy Cronin that the real Mandela had been killed in prison, that his lookalike had been 'trained for years by the Boers' and 'released' in 1990 to hoodwink blacks and protect whites.[109] Twenty years later, and in a different register, Siki Mgabadeli is a well-known face and influential voice in the new South Africa: she is the leading financial journalist on national television and host of radio talkshows. In 2013 she told a British academic, 'in 1994, we were marketed as the "Rainbow Nation" like a fancy commodity in an ad. But in truth, Mandela was too preoccupied with white fears and not enough with black grievances and expectations of a better life ... from the onset Mandela was too timorous.'[110]

Versions of this critique are clearly audible among African students and intellectuals. As historical explanation they are inadequate, a mirror image of the over-attribution of credit to Mandela for bringing about a democratic South Africa. The criticism – 'he sold us out' or 'he tried too hard to please whites' – personalises a much more complex and plural accommodation by the ANC with the interests of capital.

The issue of whether and to what extent he may have 'sold out' is relevant when it comes to a historical assessment of Mandela as president. As noted earlier, Mandela personified the ANC's lurch towards the right on economic matters, and he used his impregnable position within the party to defend the newfound fiscal orthodoxy. This in turn imposed real constraints on his government's policy choices. Despite his personal probity, his loyalty to his comrades, and the poor judgement that this often represented, saw corruption take root during his term of office. Two of the concepts most closely associated with Mandela himself – the need for forgiveness and reconciliation, and the oneness of a Rainbow Nation – did not survive his presidency. Not only were the findings of the Truth and Reconciliation Commission challenged in court by Mandela's two deputy vice presidents, de Klerk and Mbeki, but the ANC chose not to implement its recommendations for reparations. The 'rainbow' commitment to non-racialism found it difficult to sink roots in the sour soil of historically racialised attitudes and prejudices. Moreover, the 1994 promise of a 'better life for all' made Mandela's ANC 'vulnerable to the cruel facts of continuing poverty and growing unemployment'.[111]

Some have argued that Mandela's most important act as president was to step down after a single term, decisively breaking an African nationalist mould of 'presidency for life' and single-party rule. Moreover, Mandela's own beliefs and political style 'engendered civic participation and democratic deliberation ... [and through] his evident delight in everyday contact with ordinary people Mandela encouraged his compatriots to behave as assertive citizens'.[112] He was far more open to criticism and debate than Presidents Mbeki and Zuma; he not only referred constantly to collective decision-making but was willing to be out-voted. His lawyerly respect for the negotiated constitution was unfeigned.

Nelson Mandela's democratic principles and practice were rooted in twin precepts. He had this 'genuine belief', said Jakes Gerwel, perhaps closer to Mandela during his years in office and in retirement than anyone, 'that human beings were essentially "good-doing beings, beings who do good"'. And, because there is good in others, it is incumbent on the individual to recognise this, to reciprocate, to do good to others.[113]

Steering by this deceptively simple moral compass, 'he put into practice in private the values he proclaimed on the public stage … he was in the habit of being generous, respectful, courteous and kind'.[114] Because of his essential decency, integrity and respect for others, he was able to charge every calculated act of political persuasion with sincerity. As a politician, Mandela yoked principle and morality to tactical and strategic gain. He was, concluded Richard Stengel, 'the most pragmatic of idealists'. More than anything else, perhaps, it is the way that his personal, private attributes suffused his public, political life that made him such a compelling figure: hard to know, easy to love. Mandela commanded extraordinary levels of both admiration and affection. It is this remarkable combination that historians, ultimately, must understand and explain.

Notes

1 Cronin, J., 'Poem for Mandela', from *Even the Dead: Poems, Parables and a Jeremiad* (David Philip, 1997), p.30.

2 Coetzee, J.M., 'On Nelson Mandela (1918–2013)', *New York Review of Books*, 9 January 2014.

3 Nixon, R., *Homelands, Harlem and Hollywood: South African Culture and the World Beyond* (Routledge, 1994), p. 176.

4 The Special A.K.A., 'Free Nelson Mandela', released 1984, lyrics by Jerry Dammers.

5 Boehmer, E., *Nelson Mandela: A Very Short Introduction* (Oxford University Press, 2008), p. 123; Lodge, T., *Mandela: A Critical Life* (Oxford University Press, 2006), p. ix.

6 Stengel, R., *Nelson Mandela, 1918–2013: Portrait of an Extraordinary Man* (Virgin, 2012), pp. 87, 89, 92, 96.

7 Cited by Boehmer, *Nelson Mandela*, pp. 115–16.

8 Lodge, *Mandela*, p. 53.

9 Sampson, A., *Mandela: The Authorised Biography* (2nd edition, HarperPress, 2011), p. 142.

10 Mandela, N., *Long Walk to Freedom* (Macdonald Purnell, 1994), p. 311.

11 Sampson, *Mandela*, p. 143. Sampson interviewed Sisulu in November 1995.

12 Ibid., p. 174.

13 Mandela, *Long Walk*, p. 311.

14 The 1965 selection was edited by Ruth First and published by Heinemann as *No Easy Walk to Freedom*; the 1978 IDAF book, with some extra material, was titled *Nelson Mandela: The Struggle is my Life*.

15 Ranchod, R., *A Kind of Magic: The Political Marketing of the ANC* (Jacana, 2013), p. 23.

16 AAM pamphlet, 1978, cited in Genevieve Klein, 'The British Anti-Apartheid Movement and Political Prisoner Campaigns, 1973–1980' *Journal of Southern African Studies* 35, 2 (2009), p.467.

17 Posel, D., '"Madiba Magic": Politics as Enchantment', in R. Barnard (ed.), *The Cambridge Companion to Nelson Mandela* (Cambridge University Press, 2014), p. 73; Tambo cited in Klein, 'The British Anti-Apartheid Movement and Political Prisoner Campaigns', pp.468–9.

18 Quotations from Sampson, *Mandela*, pp. 333, 334, 347; Mandela, *Long Walk*, pp. 516–7.

19 Gurney, C., 'In the Heart of the Beast: The British Anti-Apartheid Movement, 1959–1994', in *The Road to Democracy in South Africa, Vol. 3: International Solidarity* (South African Democracy Education Trust, 2008), pp. 255–352.

20 Such entries in the desk calendars are reproduced in Mandela, N., *Conversations with Myself* (Macmillan, 2011), pp. 277–80, 283, 286–9, 292–3, 309.

21 Verne Harris quoted in Battersby, J., 'Afterword: Living Legend, Living Statue', in Sampson, *Mandela*, p. 609; Posel, 'Madiba Magic', p. 74; Sampson, *Mandela*, p. 398; Harris, in Battersby, 'Afterword', p. 610.

22 We Jojo, N., 'Ah! Rolihlahla!!', from Richard Bartlett (ed.), *Halala Madiba: Nelson Mandela in Poetry* (Aflame Books, 1989), p.148.

23 Mandela, *Long Walk*, p. 14.

24 Mandela, *Conversations*, pp. 8–9 (the book contains several excerpts from a proposed sequel to *Long Walk*; the text is to be completed by others and expected to be published in 2016).

25 Glaser, C., *The ANC Youth League* (Jacana Media, 2012), pp. 29–30, 36–40.

26 Meredith, M., *Nelson Mandela: A Biography* (Hamish Hamilton, 1997), p. 66.

27 Sampson, *Mandela*, p. 35; Meer, I., *A Fortunate Man* (Zebra Press, 2002), p. 80.

28 Bonner, P., 'The Antinomies of Nelson Mandela', in Barnard, *Cambridge Companion*, p. 40.

29 Tambo, O., 'Introduction', in Nelson Mandela, *No Easy Walk to Freedom* (Heinemann, 1965), p. 11.

30 Bernstein, R., *Memory Against Forgetting* (Viking, 1999), p. 116; Mandela, *Long Walk*, pp. 110, 112, 165.

31 Dubow, S., *Apartheid, 1948–1994* (Oxford University Press, 2014), p. 65.

32 Posel, D., 'The Apartheid Project', in R. Ross, A.K. Mager and B. Nasson (eds), *Cambridge History of South Africa, Vol. 2: 1885–1994* (Cambridge University Press, 2011), p. 347.

33 Cited in Lodge, *Mandela*, p.145.

34 Bonner, 'Antinomies of Nelson Mandela', p. 38.

35 The Communist Party of South Africa – CPSA – banned in 1950, reconstituted itself underground in 1953 as the SACP.

36 Mandela, *Long Walk*, p. 150.

37 Sampson, *Mandela*, p. 78.

38 Mandela, *Long Walk*, p. 200.

39 Lodge, *Mandela*, p. 145.

40 Meer, F., *Higher than* Hope (Skotaville, 1988), p. 111; Mandela, W., *Part of My Soul* (Penguin, 1985), pp. 59–65.

41 Ellis, S., 'The Genesis of the ANC's Armed Struggle in South Africa 1948–61', *Journal of Southern African Studies*, 37, 4 (2011), pp. 657–76; Malan, R., 'Mandela's Secret History', www.politicsweb.co.za/news-and-analysis/mandelas-secret-history, 16 August 2011.

42 Hepple, B., *Young Man with a Red Tie: A Memoir of Mandela and the Failed Revolution, 1960–63* (Jacana, 2013), p. 106; letter to *London Review of Books*, 23 January 2014; see also Harris, V., '"I am not a Marxist", he Said. Did he Lie?' *Mail & Guardian*, 17–23 January 2014.

43 Quoted in Lodge, *Mandela*, p. 101.

44 The text of the speech is in Mandela, N., *The Struggle is My Life* (Pathfinder Press, 1990; first published 1986), quotations at pp. 134, 153, 156–7, 160.

45 First, R., *117 Days* (Bloomsbury, 1988; first published 1965), p. 134.

46 Especially Joffe, J., *The State vs. Nelson Mandela* (Oneworld, 2007), first published as *The Rivonia Story* (Mayibuye Books, 1995); Broun, K.S., *Saving Nelson Mandela: The Rivonia Trial and the Fate of South Africa* (Oxford University Press, 2012); also all major Mandela biographies and numerous memoirs of those involved. Quotation from Joffe, *The State*, p. 24.

47 Shakespeare, W., *Julius Caesar*, Act II, Scene ii, ll. 1008–13.

48 Schalkwyk, D., *Hamlet's Dreams: The Robben Island Shakespeare* (The Arden Shakespere, 2013), p. 27.

49 Incomparably the best single account is Buntman, F., *Robben Island and Prisoner Resistance to Apartheid* (Cambridge University Press, 2003); for the early years see also Alexander, N., *Robben Island Dossier 1964–1974* (University of Cape Town Press, 1994); there are numerous memoirs and biographies. Mandela's autobiography has 180 pages on his prison years.

50 These debates are analysed in Soudien, C., 'Nelson Mandela, Robben Island and the Imagination of a New South Africa', *Journal of Southern African Studies*, 41, 2 (2015), pp. 353–66.

51 Alexander, *Robben Island Dossier*, pp. 12–14.

52 Mandela, *Long Walk*, p. 372.

53 In O'Malley, P., *Shades of Difference: Mac Maharaj and the Struggle for South Africa* (Viking, 2007), p. 161.

54 Buntman, *Robben Island*, p.92.

55 Kathrada, A., *Letters from Robben Island* (Mayibuye Books and Michigan State University Press, 1999), p. 269.

56 Kathrada, A., *Memoirs* (Zebra Press, 2004), p. 237.

57 The report is printed in full in Karis, T. and Gerhart, G., *From Protest to Challenge, Vol. 5: Nadir and Resurgence 1964–1979* (Indiana University Press, 1997), pp. 406–11.

58 Paragraph based on O'Malley, *Shades of Difference*, p. 154; Meredith, *Nelson Mandela*, p. 294; *The Road to Democracy: South Africans Telling Their Stories*, 'Andrew Mandla Masondo' (SADET, 2008), p. 262.

59 I have described these events more fully in Bundy, C., *Govan Mbeki* (Jacana, 2012), pp. 126–31.

60 Quotations from Sampson, *Mandela*, p. 276; Buntman, *Robben Island*, p. 116.

61 Quotations from Buntman, *Robben Island*, p. 124; Mandela, *Long Walk*, p. 471.

62 Sampson, *Mandela*, p.288.

63 Kathrada, *Memoirs*, p. 206; Buntman, *Robben Island*, p. 78.

64 Meredith, *Mandela*, p.289.

65 Mandela, *Conversations*, p. 172.

66 *Ibid.*, pp. 183, 191.

67 Maharaj, M. (ed.), *Reflections in Prison* (Zebra, 2001), p. 5; O'Malley, *Shades of Difference*, p. 163; Richard Stengel, R., *Nelson Mandela: Portrait of an Extraordinary Man* (Virgin, 2012), pp. 17, 19.

68 Schalkwyk, D., 'Mandela, the Emotions, and the Lessons of Prison', in Barnard, *Cambridge Companion*, pp. 57, 66; Meredith, *Mandela*, p. 1; Meer, *Higher than Hope*, p. 233.

69 Sampson, *Mandela*, p. 499.

70 O'Malley, *Shades of Difference*, p. 162; Brand, C., *My Prisoner, My Friend* (John Blake Publishing, 2014), pp. 25–6.

71 Dingake, M., *My Fight Against Apartheid* (Kliptown Books, 1987), p. 221.

72 Mandela, N., 'Clear the Obstacles and Confront the Enemy', in M. Maharaj (ed.), *Reflections in Prison* (Zebra & Robben Island Museum, 2001), p. 17.

73 Heaney, S., from 'Chorus', *The Cure at Troy* from Bartlett, *Halala Madiba*, p.186.

74   See Sparks, A., *Tomorrow is Another Country: The Inside Story of South Africa's Negotiated Revolution* (Struik, 1994); Esterhuyse, W., *End Game: Secret Talks and the End of Apartheid* (Tafelberg, 2012); Giliomee, H., *The Last Afrikaner Leaders* (Tafelberg, 2012); Barnard, N., *Secret Revolution: Memoirs of a Spy Boss* (Tafelberg, 2015); see also Mandela's *Long Walk to Freedom* and biographies by Sampson, Meredith and Lodge.

75   Mandela, *Long Walk*, pp. 513–14.

76   Giliomee, *Last Afrikaner Leaders*, p. 271.

77   These meetings are described in detail by Esterhuyse, *End Game.*

78   Gerhart, G. and Glaser, C., *From Protest to Challenge: Vol. 6, Challenge and Victory 1980–1990* (Indiana University Press, 2010), p. 146.

79   Giliomee, *Last Afrikaner Leaders*, p.318.

80   Paragraph based on Carlin, J., *Knowing Mandela* (Atlantic Books, 2013), pp. 18, 21, 27, 28.

81   Carlin, J., *Playing the Enemy: Nelson Mandela and the Game that Made a Nation* (Atlantic, 2008), p. 90.

82   Sitas, A., *The Mandela Decade, 1990–2000* (UNISA Press, 2010), p. 16.

83   Paragraph draws on Nixon, *Homelands*, pp. 186–8 and Lodge, *Mandela*, pp. 196–8.

84   Saul, J. and Bond, P., *South Africa: The Present as History* (James Currey, 2014), p.224.

85   Adam, H., Slabbert, V.Z. and Moodley, K., *Comrades in Business: Post-Liberation Politics in South Africa* (Tafelberg, 1997), p. 69.

86   Freund, B., 'The Shadow of Nelson Mandela, 1918–2013', *Review of African Political Economy*, 40, 140, p. 293; Posel, D., '"Madiba Magic": Politics as Enchantment', in Barnard, *Cambridge Companion*, p. 72.

87   Gevisser, M., *The Dream Deferred: Thabo Mbeki* (Jonathan Ball, 2007), p. xxviii.

88   Sampson, *Mandela*, p. 501.

89   La Grange, Z., *Good Morning, Mr Mandela* (Penguin, 2014), p. 86.

90   The phrase is from Johnston, A., *Inventing the Nation: South Africa* (Bloomsbury, 2014); see especially Chapter 3, 'Improvising the Nation: 1990–6'.

91   Posel, 'Madiba Magic', p. 87; Alexander, N., *An Ordinary Country* (UKZN Press, 2002), p. 53.

92   Quoted in Sampson, *Mandela*, p. 447.

93   Suzman, quoted in Sampson, *Mandela*, p. 251; Kraft, S., 'Mandela: Shattering of an Illusion', *Los Angeles Times*, 8 March 1989.

94   Quoted in Meredith, *Mandela*, p.539.

95 La Grange, *Good Morning*, p. 74.

96 Cronin, J., 'Five Thoughts Concerning the Question: "What Happens After Mandela Goes?"' in *Even the Dead*, p.29.

97 Leon, T., *On the Contrary: Leading the Opposition in a Democratic South Africa* (Jonathan Ball, 2008), pp. 279–80.

98 Meredith, *Nelson Mandela*, p. 576.

99 La Grange, *Good Morning*, p.138.

100 Wonderfully recounted in Gevisser, *Dream Deferred*, pp. 697–726.

101 La Grange, *Good Morning*, p.247.

102 Beresford, D., Mandela obituary, *Guardian*, 6 December 2013.

103 Details based on Battersby, 'Living Legend', pp. 597, 607.

104 La Grange, *Good Morning*, p. 303.

105 Munusamy, R., 'Mandla Mandela and the Chamber of Secrets', *Daily Maverick,* 5 July 2013.

106 *Mail & Guardian*, 13 June 2013.

107 Krog, A., *Conditional Tense* (Seagull Books, 2013), p. 260.

108 Mashilo, A., Statement on behalf of SACP, 6 December 2013, www.politicsweb.co.za/party/nelson-mandela-was-a-member-of-our-cc-at-the-time-.

109 Cronin, J. 'Is Nelson Mandela for Real?' *Work in Progress*, number 87 (March 1993), p.15.

110 Quoted by Smith, S., 'Mandela: Death of a Politician', *London Review of Books*, 9 January 2014.

111 Paragraph draws on Sitas, *Mandela Decade*, p. 23.

112 Lodge, T., 'Nelson Mandela: Assessing the Icon', www.opendemocracy.net/article/democracy_power/africa/nelson-mandela-at-90, 18 July 2008.

113 Higgins, J., 'Living Out our Differences: An Interview with Jakes Gerwel', in P. Vale and E. Prinsloo (eds), *The New South Africa at Twenty* (UKZN Press, 2014), p. 98. Gerwel was director-general of Mandela's office while he was president and chaired the Nelson Mandela Foundation after his retirement.

114 Carlin, *Knowing Mandela*, p. 108.

Abbreviations

AAM   the (UK) Anti-Apartheid Movement
ANC   African National Congress
DP   Democratic Party
GEAR   Growth, Employment and Development Programme
GNU   Government of National Unity
MK   Umkhonto we Sizwe (the ANC's guerrilla army)
NIS   National Intelligence Service
NP   National Party
PAC   Pan Africanist Congress
RDP   Reconstruction and Development Programme
SACP   South African Communist Party
SATIS   South Africa: The Imprisoned Society (a UK-based group formed
        in 1974 under the auspices of the British AAM which focused on
        political prisoners)
UDF   United Democratic Front
YL   Youth League

A Note on Terminology

South African terminology is a minefield for the unwary. Under apartheid every South African was registered as belonging to one of four 'races': African, coloured, Indian and white. (The Population Registration Act of 1950 designated Africans 'Natives'; their official designation subsequently became Bantu, then Black. In contemporary South Africa they are often referred to as 'Black African'.) I use the term 'black' to signify African, coloured and Indian people, as a shorthand for all formerly disenfranchised groups. Otherwise I use the terms African, coloured, Indian and white when it is necessary to identify people or communities in a society where such descriptions profoundly affected people's identities and lives.

Timeline

1918	18 July: born at Mvezo, Thembuland, Transkei
1922(?)	Moves with mother to Qunu, Thembuland, Transkei
1929/30	Moves to Mqhekezweni, as ward of Thembu regent
1935–8	Completes secondary schooling at Clarkebury and Healdtown
1939	Registers for BA degree, University College of Fort Hare
1940	November: expelled from Fort Hare
1941	Travels to Johannesburg; meets Walter Sisulu, registers to complete BA degree by correspondence
1943	Commences articled clerkship; enrols for Bachelor of Laws (LLB) studies, University of Witwatersrand; marches in support of Alexandra bus boycott
1944	April: elected to ANC Youth League (YL) executive at YL's formation. October: marries Evelyn Mase
1948	National Party (NP) wins general election, having campaigned on apartheid
1950	February: becomes a member of ANC National Executive Committee. September: elected president of ANC YL
1952	Passes attorney's professional examinations and opens legal practice: 26 June: ANC launches Defiance Campaign. November: convicted for role in Defiance Campaign; receives suspended sentence; banned under Suppression of Communism Act
1955	26–7 June: Congress of the People and adoption of Freedom Charter
1956	5 December: arrested and charged (with 155 others) with treason
1958	March: divorces Evelyn. June: marries Winifred (Winnie) Nomzamo Madikizela
1960	21 March: Sharpeville massacre. 8 April: ANC and PAC banned; is detained under State of Emergency regulations but continues to appear in Treason Trial
1961	25 March: addresses All In Africa conference, Pietermaritzburg; calls for national constitutional convention. 29 March: acquitted of treason; leaves home

	and goes underground. October–November: involved in preparations for MK activities; moves to Liliesleaf Farm in Rivonia. 16 December: MK launches sabotage campaign
1962	January–July: travels extensively in Africa; visits London; commences military training in Ethiopia. 24 July: returns to South Africa. 5 August: is arrested outside Howick, Natal. October: tried for incitement and leaving country illegally; conducts own defence; is sentenced to five years' imprisonment, taken to Pretoria Central Prison
1963	Is 'Accused No. 1' in Rivonia Trial
1964	20 April: delivers statement ('an ideal for which I am prepared to die') from dock. 12 June: sentenced to life imprisonment, flown to Robben Island
1969	May: Winnie arrested and held for eighteen months. July: death of Thembi, his eldest son
1969–75	Tensions within ANC leadership on Robben Island
1976	16 June: Soweto youth revolt begins
1977	May: Winnie banished to Brandfort
1982	Is moved to Pollsmoor Prison, Cape Town, together with four other Rivonia men
1985	January: rejects President Botha's conditional offer of release
1987	Series of meetings with Coetsee, Minister of Justice
1988	Series of meetings with special committee constituted by Coetsee: 'talks about talks'. December: moved to Victor Verster prison, Paarl.
1989	July and December: meets with President Botha and his successor F.W. de Klerk
1990	2 February: de Klerk announces unbanning of ANC and other organisations, imminent release of Mandela and intention to negotiate. 11 February: is released from Victor Verster; addresses crowd in central Cape Town. 2–4 May: first formal talks between ANC and NP government
1991	July: elected ANC president at national conference in Durban
1991–93	Talks between ANC, NP and other parties proceed; extensive overseas travel winning financial and diplomatic support for ANC
1992	April: announces separation from Winnie

1993	December: with de Klerk, joint winner of Nobel Peace Prize
1994	27–8 April: General Election on basis of universal suffrage; ANC wins 62.6 per cent of vote. 10 May: sworn in as president
1996	March: divorce from Winnie finalised. June: ANC adopts GEAR as macro-economic policy
1998	Marries Graca Machel on eightieth birthday
1999	After general election, retires as president and is succeeded by Thabo Mbeki
1999–2004	Very active retirement with extensive international travel, involved in peace-making process in Burundi
2007	Visits London for unveiling of statue in Parliament Square
2008	July: in London for ninetieth birthday, fundraising events; last overseas visit
2010	July: final public appearance, closing ceremony of football World Cup
2013	5 December: dies in hospital in Johannesburg. 15 December: is buried in Qunu

Further Reading

Asmal, Kader, Chidester, David and James, Wilmot (eds), *Nelson Mandela In His Own Words: From Freedom to the Future* (Abacus, 2013, first published 2003)

Barnard, Rita (ed.), *The Cambridge Companion to Nelson Mandela* (Cambridge University Press, 2014)

Boehmer, Elleke, *Nelson Mandela: A Very Short Introduction* (Oxford University Press, 2006)

Buntman, Fran, *Robben Island and Prisoner Resistance to Apartheid* (Cambridge University Press, 2003)

Carlin, John, *Knowing Mandela* (Atlantic Books, 2013)

Dubow, Saul, *The African National Congress* (Sutton, 2003)

Gilbey, Emma, *The Lady: Life and Times of Winnie Mandela* (Vintage, 2004)

Harris, Verne (ed.), *A Prisoner in the Garden: The Opneing of Nelson Mandela's Prison Archive* (Nelson Mandela Foundation, 2004)

Joffe, Joel, *The State vs. Nelson Mandela* (OneWorld, 2007, first published 1995)

La Grange, Zelda, *Good Morning, Mr Mandela* (Allen Lane, 2014)

Lodge, Tom, *Mandela: A Critical Life* (Oxford University Press, 2006)

Maharaj, Mac and Kathrada, Ahmed (eds), *Mandela: The Authorised Portrait* (Bloomsbury, 2006)

Mandela, Nelson, *Conversations with Myself* (Macmillan, 2010)

Mandela, Nelson, *Long Walk To Freedom* (Macdonald Purnell, 1994)

Mandela, Nelson, *The Struggle is My Life* (IDAF Publications, 1990, 3rd revised edition, first published 1978)

Mandela, Winnie, *Part of My Soul* (Penguin, 1985, first published in German, 1984)

Meer, Fatima, *Higher than Hope: 'Rolihlahla We Love You'* (Skotaville, 1988)

Meredith, Martin, *Nelson Mandela: A Biography* (Simon & Schuster, 2010, new edition, first published 1997)

Sampson, Anthony, *Mandela: The Authorised Biography* (HarperPress, 2011, new edition, first published 1999)

Smith, David J., *Young Mandela* (Phoenix, 2011, first published 2010)

Stengel, Richard, *Nelson Mandela: Portrait of an Extraordinary Man* (Virgin, 2012, first published 2010)

Web Links

The key site is that of the Nelson Mandela Foundation:

www.nelsonmandela.org

In particular, see its Centre of Memory:

www.nelsonmandela.org/index.php/memory/index.php/

And important collections of interviews and speeches in the next three links:

www.nelsonmandela.org/index.php/memory/resources/speeches/

www.nelsonmandela.org/omalley/

www.pbs.org/wgbh/pages/frontline/shows/mandela/interviews

Among many other sites worth exploring are:

www.sahistory.org.za

www.sahistory.org.za/pages/people/special%20projects/mandela/menu.htm

www.apartheidmuseum.org/

www.anc.org.za/ancdocs/history/

www.anc.org.za/people/mandela

www.bbc.co.uk/search?q=nelson%20mandela

www.thewrap.com/nelson-mandela-5-great-interviews-life-legend-video/